WAYS
AND
CROSSWAYS

WAYS AND CROSSWAYS

BY

PAUL CLAUDEL

TRANSLATED BY THE REV.
FR. JOHN O'CONNOR

WITH THE COLLABORATION OF
THE AUTHOR

KENNIKAT PRESS, INC./PORT WASHINGTON, N. Y.

First Published in October 1933
Reissued in 1968 by Kennikat Press
Library of Congress Catalog Card No: 68-15820

Manufactured in the United States of America

ESSAY AND GENERAL LITERATURE INDEX REPRINT SERIES

TO

G. K. CHESTERTON

IN TOKEN OF ADMIRATION

CONTENTS

RELIGION AND POETRY

RELIGION AND POETRY[1]

I am deeply touched by the honour which you have done me in asking me to speak to you to-day not far from the tomb of Poe, in this fair city which is the metropolis of the Faith and of Catholic tradition in America; in this country hallowed by the name of our Blessed Mother.[2]

My subject will be "French Poetry," and the reason why I think Poetry should be more intimately associated with religion than it has been in the past.

Catholic means universal, and the first article of our Creed teaches us that the Universe is made up of two parts—things seen and things unseen. In things unseen we are taught by the lights of reason and of Faith. In the visible things we are taught by the lights of reason, imagination, and sense. All these things are very good according to their order. Reason is good. Imagination is good. Sensitiveness is good. Only heretics or Jansenists, like Pascal, are capable of believing that any

[1] Conference given in English to the Catholic Societies of Baltimore, November 14th, 1927.

It resumes and develops in an original manner certain ideas already put forth in the letter to the *Figaro*, in 1914, and the introduction to the work of Dante published in *Positions et Propositions*, Paris, 1927.

[2] Baltimore is the principal city of the state of Maryland where the two ships of Lord Baltimore, *The Ark* and *The Dove*, have carried, not in vain, the seeds of truth and freedom.

faculty of this human spirit which has been created by God, is evil in itself. Nothing is bad but abuse and disorder.

Visible things must not be sundered from things invisible. Both together make up the Universe of God and have mutual relationships clear or mysterious; indeed, the Apostle tells us that by the one we are guided to a knowledge of the others. Science is concerned only with " things visible." Her business is to go from the effect to the cause, from one material thing to another material thing; from the fact to the measurement. Her concern is with what things are, not with what they signify. Of human faculties it utilises principally the reason—reason fed by memory, and stimulated by the imagination. It is a power of ascertaining, not a power of creation. Science endeavours to classify, to systematise, and to utilise what is round about us, and thus she has no need to bring into play all the faculties of the human mind, soul and body, intelligence and heart. It is quite a different matter to see a thing and to do it. And the proper domain of Art and Poetry is, as its name connotes, to *make*. Out of a thing perceived by sense, man makes something which reason can understand and feeling can enjoy; of a material thing he makes a spiritual entity. To give the word its full meaning for our mind and for our senses, Poetry is, as you say in English, the power which fully realises beings—which transmutes them into realities. In order to know a thing you have only to understand what it is, but to *make* a thing you have to understand how it is made, and to understand how it is made, you must understand the end for which it has been made, its relationships with other beings, and the idea of Him Who in the beginning made all.

If you do not understand a thing, you have no means of making proper use of it; if you do not understand what it was intended to signify and to do, you do not understand its position in the general commonweal of things visible and invisible; if you have not a universal idea of it, if you have not a Catholic idea of it.

Of course, even without a general idea of earth or heaven, you may make very nice poetry, you may carve delicate works of art, you may put together very curious and interesting trinkets. But in this pagan poetry, there is always, it seems to me, something wizened and hampered. For the simple flight of a butterfly you need a whole sky. You cannot understand a daisy in the grass if you do not understand the sun among the stars.

French Poetry in the seventeenth and eighteenth centuries was simply a concise, witty and harmonious way of expressing thought. It was a manner of speaking in proverbs and striking sentences rather in the style of country folk. In the nineteenth century it was true poetry all right, but it was poetry without God. Many French poets of the nineteenth century had talent and even genius, but they had not the faith; and if their work gives some people the impression of a rubble heap, I would like to show you that the cause of this rapid declension is not that they lacked talent, but that they lacked religion, that is to say that in their talent and their work an essential ingredient was wanting.

To illustrate what I am putting forward, I will take some themes, or as we say *motifs* of French poetry (I might just as well say of English poetry) during the nineteenth century.

The best of these themes, because it is founded in all truth upon human nature, is that of *Revolt*. So long as there is injustice in this world, revolt is a feeling which will wake a wide and deep echo in the souls of men. It is a perfectly natural feeling, and we can even say that it is a legitimate feeling. After all we all know that man has something to say in self-defence. In that wonderful book from which the Church has taken the nine lessons of the Office of the Dead, Job speaks to his Creator quite free and fearless, and when his frightened friends endeavour to stop him, the Almighty Himself says to them: "You are fools; let the man set forth his cause in peace." Thus the best poetry of the nineteenth century is a poetry of revolt. And yet revolt has one great, artistic disadvantage. It leads nowhere. It leaves you exactly where you were when you began, and since it is vain, it is tiring and soon becomes tiresome. It stirs us to beat the air. Moreover, the best poetic themes are those which I call composing themes, themes which, like nature, need for self-expression a great variety of elements. Well, revolt is not a composing theme. It does not make things harmonious, because its object is none other than disorder. A piercing shriek of protest may reach the heart, it will never create harmony.

Akin to the theme of revolt are *despair* and *cynicism*, both largely drawn upon by the poetry of the past century: good or tolerable verse has been made in this vein. But they are open to the same criticism. Despair is a passing disposition. The soul of man was never made for that. Cynicism is sometimes amusing, but it is second-rate, and we are quickly " fed up " with it. We cannot build anything with materials like revolt, despair, nihilism, cynicism, nor any of these purely negative ideas. Here I will indulge in a little footnote. When freedom of thought was won at the outset of the last century, when the ancient bonds of dogma and superstition were shattered, one would have naturally expected a perfect inundation of joy. A man, who after long years of captivity, gets back his liberty, generally feels wild with joy. Now is it not a striking thing to find that in the whole of the poetry of the nineteenth century, joy is conspicuous by its absence? You sometimes find a gross delight in the lowest pleasures, but when you look for joy, you find only despair, blasphemy, home-sickness for lost purity, and regret for the shattered bonds. In my opinion, the greatest French poet of the nineteenth century is Baudelaire, because he was very intelligent, and very well understood what he was about. Yes, Baudelaire is the greatest French poet of the nineteenth century, because he is the poet of Remorse.

In a century French poetry went through the whole gamut of paganism, and passed from the wild dreams of the revolution and romanticism to the nihilism, the materialism, and the utter despair of those years which are not very far removed from the present.

But, we are told, outside religion there are still constructive themes. Here is one for instance: the immortality of the soul, everyone knows, has been discredited by Science. After death the soul disappears entirely like a puff of smoke, but is it not a comforting thought that our dear body goes on existing in the winds, in the sunshine, in the flowers, and the little birds? You know this theme. It has given rise to oceans of bad verse, because you cannot make good poetry out of a silly notion. This theme is not good, nor partly good. It is asinine. Two minutes reflection is enough to show us that even if matter survives, ourselves do not, which after all, is the only thing that matters. It is not the same thing whether the Venus de Milo survives as a statue or as paving stones. It is not the same thing if a rose survives as a rose or as leaf mould.

Let us take another so-called constructive theme: Evolution. I do not mean evolution as a scientific doctrine. I do not know whether it be true or false—it is all the same to me—and personally, I do not believe in it, because nothing can be two things at the same time. I consider it here only as a poetic idea, as a stimulant to the mind in composing something. At first blush, evolution appears as a vitalising idea, and full of promise, because it implies change and gives freer rein to fancy. I suppose that evolution has been of great help to novelists, and besides, I think personally, that most books on evolution are nothing more than romances, second-rate fairy-tales. But what so-called poets have tried to do with evolution has not been a success. I remember several hotchpotches, epic and didactic, which the poor misguided but well-meaning builders like René Ghil or Louis Bouilhet have endeavoured to write round the adventures of Brother Diplodocus in the land of Lias. The result was dreadful. As a holiday task I myself once set to write for my children an address of congratulation presented by all the animals to Sister Giraffe on the day when after long ages of fossil endeavour she managed to add sixteen vertebræ to her spine. I could read it to you, but I do not want to discourage you from certain perfectly lawful ambitions of the same Giraffic order. True, the Gospel tells us that we cannot add one cubit to our stature. But St. Matthew is quite a poor fellow beside Mr. Wells or simple Mr. Lamarck.

To return to my subject, I think evolution a bad theme because a poet likes to take seriously everything about him. He does not look upon them as trial sketches intended to be supplemented forthwith by brand new creations (just as you talk about a " Creation " of Mayol at the Café-Concert or a " Creation " of La Samaritaine or of the Galeries Lafayette).

He looks on things as figures of Eternity, figures full of joy and inexhaustible teaching and of immense importance. He sees nothing to change in them: he detests the idea of seeing them changed. Eternity would not be long enough for him to apprehend them. Nature for him is like a man who says the same thing over and over, as if that something were of considerable importance. The same rose and the same violet will always be the same because from the beginning they have been very good—*valde bona*, and cannot be better. Rose and violet can only become a better rose or a better violet than they are already.

I could show you many other out-moded poetic themes which have fallen into ruin like this. It is rather saddening to see how little time it takes for a new fashion to fade and grow ridiculous. Remember what happened to Tolstoy, to Nietzsche, to Ibsen. Even in the splendid dramas of Wagner, when Erda begins to utter oracles, we cannot keep back a smile or a yawn. The poetry of Wagner is like the Rhine flowing among the ancient burgs and ruined castles, or what is sadder still, castles restored in the Kaiser Wilhelm taste. The buildings give you a pain, but beneath them the Rhine flows for ever.

For things and for poems, there is but one way of being new, and that is to be true; there is only one way of being young, and that is to be eternal.

And this brings me to the conclusion of my lecture, which is to point out to you some immense advantages which religion brings to poetry. I do not say that every good Catholic is also a good poet, because poetic talent, poetic inspiration, is like prophecy, a grace—an unearned grace, or, as theologians say, *gratia gratis data* (a grace given for its own sake); but I believe that the Catholic poet has in some points an immense advantage over his fellow poets.

I will give three examples of the particular way in which religion can help poetry.

The first is that Faith in God allows of *Praise*. Praise

is perhaps the greatest mover of poetry, because it is the expression of the deepest need of the soul, the voice of joy and life, the business of all creation wherein every creature has need of every other. Great poetry from the Vedic Hymns to the Canticle of the Sun of St. Francis is a single hymn of praise. Praise is the creative theme *par excellence*. Nobody sings alone. Even the stars of heaven, we read in the sacred books, sing together.

Religion gives us not only song, it gives us speech as well. Religion (the Christian Religion—the Catholic Religion, it is all one to me), has given the world not only joy but *meaning*.

Since we know that the world is not the work of chance, of blind natural forces groping after one another, we know that it must have a meaning. It bespeaks its Creator: it gives us the means to understand His work or anyhow to question Him and pay Him our dues. It leads us towards Him by many wondrous ways. It gives us the means of asking and replying, of learning and of teaching, of doing good to our brethren, and receiving it from them.

You see all about you sceptics and agnostics, who, like half-wits are powerless to answer the simplest moral or intellectual questions. A Catholic knows what is black and what is white; to every question he can answer yes, or no, a full clear yes, and a resounding no. All these things are priceless to a poet and to an artist, because scepticism, doubt, hesitation, are just the deadly cancer of true art.

The third advantage religion gives us is Drama. In a

world where you do not know the yes or the no of anything, where there is no law, moral or intellectual, where everything is lawful, where there is nothing to hope and nothing to lose, where evil brings no punishment, and good no recompense—in such a world there is no drama, because there is no struggle, and there is no struggle because there is nothing worth the trouble. But with Christian Revelation, with the enormous unbounded ideas of heaven and hell, which are as much above our comprehension as the starry sky is above our heads, human actions, human destiny are invested with prodigious value. We can do an infinite good or an infinite evil. We have to find our way guided or misguided like the Homeric heroes by unseen friends or foes, among the most exciting and unforeseen vicissitudes towards sunlit peaks or to darkling deeps of misery. We are like the actors in a very interesting drama written by an author, infinitely wise and good, in which we play an essential part, but in which it is impossible for us to know beforehand the least turn of the plot. For us life is always fresh and always interesting, because every moment we have something new to learn, and something necessary to achieve. The last act, as Pascal says, is always gory, but always magnificent as well, for religion has not only brought drama into life, it has set to its ending in death the highest form of drama, which for every disciple of our Divine Master is *sacrifice.*

DISCOURSE TO THE CATHOLIC ACTORS OF NEW YORK

DISCOURSE TO THE CATHOLIC ACTORS OF NEW YORK

Ladies and Gentlemen,

Thus kindly invited to speak at your Annual Meeting, from my two-fold quality of dramatic author and diplomat, I derive both confidence and ill-ease. With your profession I have relations now of long standing, and they have left me none but pleasant recollections. There are few artists, and I say it in all sincerity, in whom one finds so much conscientiousness, so much devotion and desire of well-doing: and all for the sake of getting in a newspaper a few lines of light-headed praise or vague criticism, if it is your good fortune to escape complete oblivion or the most deathly misunderstanding. Besides, has not my trade of diplomat certain resemblances to yours? Are we not both in a perpetual state of representation, saddled with a part in a play, of which the scenario and the movement have been regulated by others than ourselves, and of which we endeavour to make the best we can?

And, moreover, is there not between the author and that child of his thought who takes advantage of the connivance of an interpreter to make insolent claim to independence, an underground rivalry which sometimes works out to irritation? And also how pretend to a place among the heroes of the apron-stage, when one's own self is one of those old gentlemen who move about dimly down there in the neighbourhood of a set ready to swallow them up again, even whilst a heartrending drama is unfolded from the walk-round to the conclusion near the footlights, where every reply has the vigour of a thrust and passion's victims are gloriously carved with great knives in the spotlight to the applause of an enraptured public?

The diplomat's trade, is it not less to act than to hinder events from developing through their virulence and to keep them shut up in the cunning trap of procedure and circumlocution until the international masses shall have had the time to get accustomed to the new relation, generally almost imperceptible, which circumstances have imposed upon them? Rather than gaily collaborating in a dramatic crescendo, is it not his part to reduce the cadence of the passions to that of everyday life, and to open to the world of the novel and unexpected which so loves to toss its plumed head in the newspapers, the mildewed haven of precedent?

Still, if one were to fancy carrying further this parallel, seemingly rather forced, between the diplomat's trade and that of the actor or dramatic author, I think that without straining ingenuity, it would be easy to find other resemblances. Too often is the diplomat's art deemed to be that of an observer whose whole business is to know the greatest possible number of facts and deduce from them the correct conclusions; to go from the known to the unknown, whether it be a lot of political or social facts or the characters of our various partners and interlocutors, by the simplest and most likely road. From this point of view the talent of the person in question should resemble that of the psychologist amusing himself with the human comedy in its endless variety of types and interlacing of motives, and making it the theme of his woven damask. Or, if you like it better, of the philosopher who out of a confused jumble makes an ordered spectacle. That is what I call taking one's place in the pit. But perhaps it is more important to the understanding of what is going on, to go up one's self upon the stage and take part in the action. In one word, diplomacy is not merely the art of questioning, it is not simply a matter of knowing the facts, but of setting things in motion and challenging the unknown.

That is a far-reaching distinction applying to the whole field of art and even of science, and to the whole universe of human activity. The men of science, who are often humbugs, try to make us believe that they come into the presence of phenomena in a condition of plasticity and absolute indifference to the result, positive or negative, which they purpose to obtain. In reality it is hardly ever that. Experience is always the consequence of an hypothesis either entirely gratuitous or based upon the most summary and arbitrary of reasonings, which is analogy. But, on the other hand, the scientist would be a very slack lover if he allowed himself to be discouraged by any denial of the truth which he is wooing. Denials for him are not defeat, they are indications which in the long run will make him free of a rebel's heart. And in

Art likewise where should we be if we rested satisfied with the data as such, and with heavy concentration limited ourselves to laying down what the naturalistic novelists of bygone times used to call in their boorish slang "a slice of life"? Like the practitioner who by touching a certain almost imperceptible point of the mucous membrane of the nose provokes a sneeze, a profound shock, a reaction of our whole nervous system, "fit" as they say "to raise the dead," in like manner the exquisite artist, musician or painter by a single well-chosen note is able to put on trial the whole order of the universe and to give it a new meaning.

Well, then! the whole cunning of a dramatic author and of his interpreters lies in this art of questioning, of finding the word, the formula, the tonality, the inflection, which will pry out from the depth of our interlocutor's soul the reply which we await. When a young person sees outlined on the screen the delightful physiognomy of Novarro and Valentino, and sees gathering together the elements of that masterful gaze, all sorts of favourable and unforeseen thoughts arise from her troubled heart. I will not compare this feeling with that of a Minister of Foreign Affairs mastering the contents of a well-drafted dispatch. And yet there is no statesman who does not recognise the importance, the authority of a well-found formula which lights up a whole dark debate and precipitates latent resolutions. A mother knew not what she possessed of tenderness, patience, ingenuity, and even physical strength, until a child came to lay claim to it all. And how many humble Napoleons has not war brought to light in the person of a joiner or a book-keeper, a café-waiter, a philologist? Behold a method in psychology far superior to the introspection and the pernickety and often silly analyses of modern novelists; it is that of everyday life, and also that of the theatre. No one knows his own deep resources, and everyone spends his life awaiting the essential question which may awaken the slumbering psyche.

This essential question, ladies and gentlemen, since you and I have the honour to be Catholics, can we say that we do not know it, that we have not heard in ourselves at least its forewarning and its echo? Is it not that of which the most searching debates of tragedy form but a travesty, that in which by a continual and veiled allusion the most cunning entanglements of the most expert dramatic engineers are consummated? We all know it, that searching question, that solemn interrogation. It is that which we hear at Baptism and which will be repeated at our last hour. It is that interpellation directly and personally addressed by name to every one of us, and which it is not possible to shirk by any way out. It is that which Our Lord addressed to the first Pope on the road to Cæsarea Philippi: "What thinkest thou of the Son of Man?"

And there is another and still older interrogation, one which God Himself formulated in the earthly paradise, when He was seeking for His work, for that Adam of His creation whom He had animated with His breath and who at the serpent's instigation had miserably endeavoured to make himself over again to his own image. This question is that which the world about us, which daily circumstances as well as metaphysical anguish or the brutal interventions of destiny or of passion unceasingly put to us:

"Adam, where art thou?"

New York, 1929.

PROPOSITIONS ON JUSTICE

PROPOSITIONS ON JUSTICE[1]

" The world is full of Christian truths run wild."
(Chesterton.)

They have cast lots upon Christ's vesture and have shared it out at random.

To go wild is to lose one's head. A truth which is no longer in its proper place in the head, a Principle, is a truth run wild. Such is the discrowned and discredited Justice which has escaped from Proudhon's book into our public places.

I. ON NEGATIVE JUSTICE

i. Justice enjoins equally what we must do and not do. It is positive and negative.

ii. The precept of negative justice is laid down in these words by the Gospel: " Do not unto others what you would not that they should do unto you."

By these words we receive a double mandate: the first, not to take from another what is his, his goods, his life, his honour; not to injure him in any way by fraud or by violence; not to leave him at a loss for the means of following out his reasonable aims.

The second, which is the consequence of the first, is to repair the damage which we have caused, to give back

[1] After reading Proudhon's book *De la justice dans la révolution et dans l'Eglise.*

what we have taken, or, if there has been free consent, what we have received from another and what is his due (*dehabitum*), that in us which is his.

iii. Justice in this sense, like the notion of God Himself, from which it borrows its commanding force and its rational value, is a principle of natural religion independent of Revelation. But we shall see that by itself alone, being purely negative, it is an insufficient basis for the relations of men among themselves.

iv. These latter in fact consist essentially in the aid which they lend one another, in the positive good which they do to one another, and not in the evil which they don't do.

But two cases may arise: either the good which we have received is the correlative of another good which we undertake to get: in this case there is contract, and justice is consummated in the carrying out of this contract or Law or sign-manual.

Or the good which we have received or brought about has been provided quite gratuitously, and without any thought of recompense on the part of the giver.

In this latter case the good which has been done us is not done in view of that other definite good which we may bring about, but for our own sake. And yet, in this case too, there is in us something which we owe to another, which belongs to him with its fruits, which is *due* to him: there is obligation, but it does not carry with it the designation of its counterpart.

v. Negative justice is not a principle of action, but of conservation and balance.

No principle of natural justice binds us to perform a gratuitous deed of goodwill towards a stranger. No justice counsels us to reply to a gratuitous good deed by an equivalent deed (for it is not this second act that has caused the first); neither to quench our obligation.

Thus negative justice is limited to the single domain of abstention or of contract. On one side there are the benefits which we have received, entirely gratuitous benefits which we never could do without, from God, from our parents, from friends, and even from society; and of which we can certainly never give back the equivalent. On the other hand no one is so poor and outcast as not to have at any moment the means of doing good to another creature without self-interest by a purely friendly gesture.

God, having received nothing from man, acts in his regard only by gift or grace, and therefore cannot be unjust to him.

vi. The consummation of negative justice consists in the quittance given by the contracting parties and not in any objective equivalent of the goods exchanged, for they are never comparable.

There is no comparison of value between the needful and the superfluous; between this bunch of flowers which I throw aside hardly smelt and the silver coin which means a day's livelihood for a whole family; between the work of a great artist and the cheque of the speculator who buys it; between the bread which is no use to the baker and the cloth which is no use to the weaver. There is always something given "into the bargain": everything is by agreement.

They are not so much values to be gauged as temptations to be resisted, mutual needs to pair off one way or another. By the exchange both parties agree simply to be rid of all further obligation. Far from tying men together justice separates them instead, and far from creating obligations she extinguishes them. The popular idea of justice is "to owe no man anything!" The highest praise: a man who owes no one anything.

vii. This kind of justice by itself would be a dead justice, for in order to be perfect it would have to consist not in the equivalent of the goods, but in the transfer of objects exactly alike. For a loaf I should have to give back a loaf, and not a similar loaf, but the same.

viii. The cause of so much stump oratory is the confusion between the idea of Justice and the idea of Justness.

Herein we leave the field of reason to enter upon that of sentiment, the measurements of seemliness being always arbitrary.

But this brings us to the second part of our proposition.

II. POSITIVE JUSTICE

i. The precept of positive justice is given us in these words of the Gospel: "Thou shalt love the Lord thy

God with thy whole heart, and with thy whole soul, and with thy whole mind, . . . and thy neighbour as thyself."

ii. Positive justice consists then in a reasonable valuation of the ends of man, and in an affection of the will agreeable with the object which it has in view. Justice is not a thing in itself, a substance. It is an instrument, a second hand, a *habitus*, a reasonable way of owning ourselves and administering our goods, of which the most precious is our intelligent soul with its power of loving.

iii. The motive for loving God above all is given us in that He is *the Law*, the Ancient of Days who has given us everything without any hope of equivalent advantage from us. Since He has given us all, it is to Him that all is due (*dehabitum*) and to Him we must render all.

iv. The motive for positive justice towards men is no longer the mere idea of the debt which binds us in regard to certain of them, but the idea of what is *due* in the sense of what is *wanting*. The debt is passive, the duty is active. We form, together with our like, a complex of complementary organs, a body, a Church: I am necessary to them all as they are all necessary to me, they challenge me to default at my peril.

v. The measure of my justice towards other men will therefore be not the measure of my obligation, but of my strength. As a fact, if God is the sole end, I cannot love myself save in relation to Him; so to love my neighbour as myself is to love him in relation to God. Thus I have an *interest* in all reasonable creatures. Whether it is myself or my neighbour, the aim is identical (*mea res agitur*): in one instance as in the other it is a question of forces which I have to utilise, a responsibility for which I am answerable, of a concert which I have to complete by providing the *right note*. I am not complete without the full scale of me. I am not complete without the gamut of all my keys, for with them I am linked by inbred, innate, and pre-established kinship.

vi. Note the term "neighbour" (*proximus:* the nearest neighbour). It is not a question merely of loving all men in general, but the nearest neighbour, those whom circumstances or nature have set down nearest to us. And who is the nearest neighbour of all? The answer to this question is the Gospel of the Good Samaritan: it is he who has most need of us.

vii. Justice then, rightly understood, is not a negative principle, a principle of death constraining to render to every man his due and so be quit of all obligation towards him. It is a principle of life and action. We must aid our neighbour according to our strength to fulfil this duty which he has of being our brother in one sole Father.

We must co-operate in this image of God which he is building up. That is why it is written: "Unless your justice abound more than that of the scribes and Pharisees you shall not enter into the Kingdom of Heaven" ; that is why the Kingdom of Goodwill and of Grace has been put in place of that of the Law : "And he hath taken the same (*i.e.*, the Law) out of the way, fastening it to the cross." (St. Paul.)

"Let your justice abound"—and indeed we see in nature that a grain of corn never produces a single grain of corn, but it either dies and rots in the place where it is cast, or it brings forth the thirty, forty, or hundred of the parable.

viii. This is the meaning of Christian justice : which is to answer *right* to what God and our neighbour expect, and that is why it is harder to be a just man than a superman.

LETTER TO SYLVANUS PITT

When I told you, dear friend, that since the Revolution "there is no longer anything freely given by man to man," I did not mean that the revolution, thank God ! had managed to change human nature and abolish all disinterested relations between man and man : I simply wished to state the principle of the new revolutionary code. You have read Proudhon's famous book, *De la justice dans la révolution et dans l'Eglise*, in which the men of the Fourth of September were steeped. You will see there that between man and man there is no room for more than justice or interest (solidarity). The very name of Charity is outlawed. It is at this doctrine that I will be the first to tilt, by showing how justice of itself is a notion inadequate and dead. Inadequate, because every man by nature has the right not to any part but to the whole. Dead, because justice would give the same thing for the same thing, a crust of bread for another crust of bread.

The shoemaker who trades a pair of shoes against a crust, trades a thing which is absolutely useless to him against another thing which is absolutely necessary. There is no justice but necessity. It is not a question of shoes or flour and other things dead and worthless by themselves : it is a question of one man who is hungry, another who is barefoot. Charity considers flesh and blood ; justice, wages : the steel needle and the iron weights. Look at nature : one grain of corn will produce thirty, forty, or a hundred grains of corn—or not at all, but never will it produce a single grain of corn (see the parable) : that is why in its splendid advent Christianity broke the scales, the codes, the swords of the old Roman Empire. It had destroyed the law (St. Paul) and had put in its stead that *grace* in the most radiant sense of the word, which the noblest hearts of ancient days had hoped for.

By grace we give our brother not only the love to which of himself he was entitled (*i.e.*, none at all most of the time), but that which we owe to God, Whose image and child he is, apart from all deserving and precisely for the very reason of this absence of all human motive. That is why St. Peter Claver goes among the negroes and Fr. Damian among the lepers. The modern revolution came to darken and degrade everything, to reduce everything to self-interest: it destroyed the rich and, what is far more horrible, it has tainted the poor.

The new revolutionary code lays down law for things dead and worthless in themselves: the ancient code regulated somehow or other, relationships between persons. Every man had his place in an immense *ritual.* To set it up again there is no need to bother with the past. We have but to re-establish the idea of God and in that soft radiance understand the value of every deed of ours. The act of a man buying a bit of bread at the baker's would become, if both knew what they were about, as grave, as solemn, as sacred, as that of two priests who after the Communion exchange the peace, laying both hands on each other's shoulders.

It may be that lay morality cannot well hinder the existence of those virtuous mediocrities who sicken both God and man. It will never give that hunger and thirst after justice as deep down, as ravenous, as devouring as material hunger, which the great saints knew: it is neither tense nor intense. "If the salt lose its savour, wherewith shall it be salted?"

ON EVIL AND LIBERTY

ON EVIL AND LIBERTY

i. *Evil*, all that is contrary to the end of a creature. *End of a creature*, that for which it is made.

Thus a bad knife is one that does not cut as it should. A bad horse is one that runs badly.

In this sense which we will call physical, the agent is not the cause of the failure of his own operation.

In the sense which we will call moral, the agent is more or less the cause of failure of his operation, whether by imperfect vision of his end, or by defect of strength, or by perverse will. So we say that a professor is bad, either through stupidity, or through mental sloth, or through an insufficient will to instruct.

Now God being the cause of all, it is concluded that He is directly the cause of evil, whether physical or moral. For the present we shall consider only moral evil.

ii. God cannot be the cause of moral evil.

In point of fact moral evil can only result as we have seen from a defect in the knowledge of the worker or insufficiency of his strength or a perverse will.

Now God being by definition, All Knowing, All-Powerful and All-Good, this triple root of ill is not in Him, for if He were Himself the cause of a defect, He would be the cause of a defect in His Perfection as craftsman. He would cease to be God since He would cease to be Perfect—as a figure is not a triangle if it has more or less than three sides.

iii. Evil not coming from God, can therefore come only from the creature, and from the intelligent and free. For if this creature were not absolutely free, absolutely seeing, absolutely cause of its own act, evil would not come from the creature itself, but from the cause determining.

iv. But these conditions could never be united except in the first man sprung straight from the Hands of God. All men later did in fact receive their being by the intermediary of another nature of which they abide part and parcel.

We see then how in our present state, although liberty exists in us, the conditions necessary to its perfect exercise are lacking: on one side a clear vision of our end, and on another the entire submission of our material nature. We find ourselves from birth laden with servitudes which are the consequences of a choice made before us and for us by the first man: in perfect freedom—that is what is called Original Sin, that is to say joined to our nature, incorporated in our existence.

v. But then why did God give man that liberty which He foresaw he would use so badly?

I answer that God could no more make a man un-free than a wheel not round. He has put into every creature a force adapted to its nature, and necessary to its operation. This force is purely material in minerals and vegetables. It is instinctive in the animal adapted to a set number of conditions of existence; it is reasonable in man who steers by general apprehension and is called to make use of the whole universe through intelligence and manipulation of causes. He who is subject to one order is not free; he who is to choose among all possible orders cannot but be free, for his choice is no longer settled by necessity, but by a reasonable good-pleasure in the best.

vi. So Original Sin is a fact which willy-nilly we must needs accept whatever be the objections against it of a shallow common sense. 'Tis vain for us to say: How can we be branded with a sin which we have not committed? We shall know how far the roots of our responsibility extend when we know how far down go the roots of our life or causating activity. The transmission of the sin is a mystery, but in the same sense as the transmission of life.

Meanwhile we submit the following considerations:

vii. Be it noted at the very outset that the bliss, which the elect redeemed by the Blood of Christ, shall enjoy in heaven, and which will in some sort endow them with divine powers, is not natural but supernatural; that between it and our nature there is a relationship not of necessity, but of fitness; that it is due not to justice but to grace.

Take the case of a roadmender breaking stones on a road: he may earn ten francs all right, a hundred francs, a thousand francs; he may earn his daily bread, but he cannot earn the crown of France. Even so, by our finite activity we can quite well earn happiness or unhappiness conformable with our nature, but not so as to become gods,—not so as to receive the "adoption of the Sons of God."

viii. In what did Original Sin consist?
It consisted in an act which started the first *heresy* or separation, that is to say, a preferring of ourselves before God.

ix. This sin had an immediate influence on the man who committed it, upon that man not only as creature, but as himself cause and origin. God made man and sin unmade him. He thus handed himself down to his descendants just as he was, unable to give them more than he was himself; that is to say, the estate of God's image, but the estate of an image of God, if I may so say, excommunicated from its model—isolated, vitiated, counterfeit. The mainspring was put out of order by him. He is apt no more to bring forth into the free air a live image of God, but to forge in that narrow house which henceforth will be his home, that idol which stands instead of God.

x. By Original Sin man has elected to stand alone. To the Paradise of God he has preferred this strait domain which he may henceforth truly call his own, since it is the garden, the field, whence he draws his substance. Man, the heir of Adam, will no more be present save to himself, save to the space adapted to his works, save in his own land, his own workshop. He will no more be attached to God save by reason, and by the light which tradition may have kept for him. The time of Vision is over, and the time of Faith begins. Thus Adam leaves to his heirs a damaged will, and a closed-in world of matter. He has said to God "I go this way—Thou that way." Since he committed the sin, he covers up that part of him whence comes the origin; he tries to hide it, to keep it away from God. It is without looking at Him that he wills to be the author of the human race. All his posterity is born on the other side of the veil and is blind.

xi. The consequence of sin is death.

Every effect whose cause is hampered, itself suffers in the measure of the hindrance. A purely physical effect disappears if its cause is kept from maintaining it. After sin, the man or image of God cannot perish, since if he could perish, he would no longer be in the image of God, but he is reft of the power of using what he receives from his causes for the construction of an image of the God from whom a veil henceforward sunders him. He is no more than a precarious idol, a rough sketch or free translation, an interpretation for the nonce. He has preferred what in him was transitory to what he had of everlasting. He counted on his own resources only, on what he draws by his own means out of the world about him which he masters. But these resources being finite, the life he draws from them through the union of his soul with material organs, is equally finite. He plunges into a stream which enriches him only to strip him naked. Things take back from him this body which they have made, which he owes to them, and which he can no longer use to image his Creator.

xii. If the soul at the moment of death is found in the domain of Original Sin, it is before God like a mechanism wound up for the finite, but which has set before it the infinite, that is to say, something which it cannot at all assimilate. It has no organs fit for God. It is like a fish with nothing but air to breathe. God therefore cannot give Himself to her, but if she has merited finite happiness He can give her a finite happiness in Limbo, knowledge without possession, a negative quietude, fairly analogous in fact to that image of Paradise to come which Buddhists and Pagans picture unto themselves.

xiii. By the Incarnation the Son of God has taken on our nature. He has given back to God the fulness of the debt which Adam had contracted. By our union with Him he has brought us to the fulness of His rights; for where the head is, there are the members also.

xiv. In the state of innocence man was united to God by what the theologians call *fides oculata*. Ransomed man is united to God through Christ, and to Christ in baptism by Faith. Christ died for us, and we die henceforth with Christ; what was punishment, with Him becomes payment and redemption. And as He is risen, we shall rise again.

xv. The sinner while he is alive, that is to say, composed of body and soul, can again unite himself wholly with Christ by penance and by faith. The man who dies in the state of sin has lost that body which he had in common with Christ, that veil in whose shelter he dwelt since Eden, and he can no longer give it up to Him. He is nothing more than a soul, evermore seeing and consequently never more meriting. And it is quite true that after the final resurrection, souls find again their body but no longer an *opaque* body. " Hell is naked before Him," says Job, " and there is no covering for destruction."

xvi. Thus Hell does not come from God, it comes from a hindrance to God on the side of the sinner.[1]

God does not hate any of His creatures; to all He goes on supplying the existence proportionate to their end, and that secret sap with which the elect compose their figure to the image of His face. But the sinner uses this inward virtue to project his own idol, his personal counterfeit of the august Sign-manual. There is therefore a contradiction between the natural longing and the essential end of every created being on one hand,

[1] " I will cause to break out of the midst of thee," says Ezekiel, " a devouring fire."

and on the other hand the violence done it by the reprobate will. Not being conscious of our formative cause here below, no more are we conscious of our deformity, but face to face with God, we shall confront in perfect light at once our cause and the deformation which is our doing; our cause and the violence which we have done it. The damned will know what it is to produce this miscarried and misshapen image—eternal self-realisation in blasphemy. There is in him a longing to be God which he can never either realise or destroy.

Every man who does not die in Christ and in communion with Him, dies in his own image. He can no longer alter the seal of himself which through every instant of his life he has stamped upon the eternal substance. So long as the word is unfinished, the hand can draw back and erase it with the Cross, but when it is ended it is indestructible like the material which has received it. "What I have written I have written."

xvii. It is commonly objected—how can a finite fault entail infinite punishment?

The question is badly put. Evil has no existence by itself, and consequently it is no more finite than it is infinite. But it can have different consequences according to the being which upholds it. If this being is mortal the evil will disappear with him; if he is immortal like the human soul he will carry away his deformities with him unless penance and grace have done away with them.

Therefore it cannot be said that the finite creature is

punished with infinity. On the contrary it is the being naturally adapted to the infinite or immortal whom his sins enclose in the finite. It is like a hard shell, a frightful encrustation, a sclerosis coming to block the organs through which the creature could maintain itself in a state of blissful give-and-take in the lap of eternal life. Only the elect can say with the Psalmist: " We have passed through fire and water " and again " Thy living creatures shall dwell therein (the sea of God's Mercy)." And again it is said: " Thy judgments are a great deep."

It is in this great deep according to his density that he will come into his place of glory or of punishment.

xviii. It remains to say a few words on physical evil.

As regards man there are no difficulties. Physical evil is the image and the consequence of sin. It is the effect of his falling away and of that dominion over natural forces which has been taken from him. It is a warning of his fault, and one of the instruments of his salvation.

But with a kind and reasonable God, how do you justify this apparent disorder of which we see the image everywhere in nature? How justify the suffering of innocent creatures like the animals? I answer that this disorder is only apparent, and that besides it is quite just that fallen man should dwell in a world which on all sides deprived of the immediate presence of its cause, offers the aspect of ruin and rough handling. Nowhere are these conditions such that man may not realise himself by reason and by labour.

As to the sufferings of animals, one must distinguish

those which are the result of the wickedness and extravagance of man, and those which are the doing of life itself. These latter exaggerated even so by our imagination are perhaps only an effect of that obscure fraternity which links together all the creatures of the one Creator. The Master could not suffer without all these lowly servants suffering with Him. We feel that it is for us they suffer.

Besides I do not believe there were no carnivorous animals in the Earthly Paradise, and that lions fed on fruit and vegetables. Their perfection lying in eating sheep, and the sheep's perfection in being eaten, they did not fail one another. And who knows if this law that creatures cannot live without devouring one another be not a dim parable of the Sacrifice and the Communion?

At Sea, Indian Ocean: September, 1921.

LETTER TO MADAME E.

Letter to Madame E.

Dear Madame,

I have found the little work I told you of, which I once wrote for a lady friend. I believe it is sufficiently clear if you read it closely and attentively.

Of course I do not pretend to have cleared up once for all these dreadful mysteries. The Church herself tells us that they are mysteries. But they are mysteries of the same kind as Regeneration, Life, the Soul, Thought, etc., that is to say, they bear the stamp of fundamental facts which we are bound to accept without understanding, and they throw light on all the rest. Evil exists and original sin is the only theory which permits us to understand to any depth its real character.

Original Sin and Hell are Fundamental Truths of the Catholic Faith. They are not episodic details of the same kind as the problem which you brought to me the other day and which may continue to be a subject of doubt without serious inconvenience. If there was no Fall, there has been no Redemption. If there is nothing to save, there was no need of a Saviour. If that Fall did not constitute an immense definite misfortune by separating us from God, the Incarnation and the Cross can have no reason. Besides, we see that on this point the Gospel and the whole Bible are absolutely clear and categoric. There is no possible way out. There is no point on which our Lord insists more emphatically and more frequently. We must believe Him or we must absolutely give up believing in Him.

The usual objections to Original Sin arise from a wrong headed notion of it. They say: "How can a man be punished for a fault that he has not himself committed?"

You will understand better if you say to yourself that this punishment is above all a *privation.*

The first man, disobeying his Author, preferred his own will to the Will of God. He preferred himself to God. He preferred his own welfare to that of God. He deliberately broke the pact which united him with his Creator. He acted, so to speak, in a revolutionary manner. He declared his independence. There was divorce. There was a break-up of the initial state of things. God withdrew His impulse, His co-operation, which was Grace; the state of commonweal and indivision with that son who pretends to have evermore attained his majority, is at an end. God gives him back his portion, that "Substance" mentioned in the Parable of the Prodigal Son, to use it at his pleasure.

(*Luke* xv. 12.)

"And the younger of them said to his father: 'Father give me the portion of substance that falleth to me'." (According to the Latin "which touches me, which belongs me, with which I am in contact") "and he divided unto them his substance."

(*Ecclesiasticus* xv. 14.)

" God made man from the beginning and left him in the hand of his own counsel. He added his Commandments and Precepts."

(*Luke* xv. 13.)

" And the younger son, gathering all together, went abroad into a far country."

(*Psalm* lxxii. 27.)

" For behold they that go far from thee shall perish: thou hast destroyed all that are disloyal to thee."

" And there wasted his substance living riotously."

Thus pride comes first, then riot.

When man thus set up in his new estate and condition, exercises his powers, he no longer exercises them in the name of God, with Whom he has rescinded his contract. He exercises them in his own name. Now among his powers is the Creative power. When he calls another being into life, he no longer calls it in the name of God, but calls it in his own name. He no longer calls it forth in the name of something Infinite; he calls it forth in the name of something finite. He no longer calls it forth in the image of God, but in the image of Adam. He cannot give him more than he has himself. He cannot give him life everlasting because it is not his to give, and because he has renounced this inheritance which has no *contingence* with him. He can only give him a finite and transitory life. He cannot give him the impossibility of sinning because that is beyond his powers. He cannot give him the power and the knowledge of God, because they are not his to give. He can but give him finite strength and light, like his own. Neither can he give the entry into Life Everlasting to that son who has been conceived outside its gates. He gives what he is. He calls forth his child no longer in the likeness of an innocent creature entirely made for God, but in that of a rebel who has taken to himself an independent *constitution*, in which all is oriented no longer towards the Sovereign Lord, but towards the proper welfare of the new estate, by the sole means of the natural strength and light which are put at his disposal.

Such is Original Sin. It has the character of an inheritance. Man transmits to man an inheritance in which all is oriented naturally towards the good of the *estate* by means of the resources placed at his disposal. Everything is made for a finite man whose end is set within himself and all is oriented towards that end.

But this conception is erroneous. Man is not an end in himself; he is not capable of himself providing an end for nature. He has that which permits nature to go right to its end which is God. In putting himself forward, in setting himself up as the end of that nature to which he has simply been made overseer, he puts himself into an abusive and violent attitude from which results the whole sequela of actual sins, like the well and what flows from it. The former is properly speaking a *privation*, the latter bears and involves a *punishment*, that is, the re-establishment of order by justice at the expense of that disorder which perturbed it.

And now to speak of Hell and those eternal pains which disquiet your tender feelings. God made man His steward over all nature. He gave it to him to cultivate and to husband so that it might yield homage unto Him. He gave it into his hands as the means of his complete self-realisation, and in order to have a sacrifice and a priest. But man, as we have seen by Original Sin, departed from God. God on one side, and man on the other. He claimed the *division*, the immediate surrender of the portion of traditional inheritance which falls to him, and by virtue of which he maintains his own existence in time. When he dies without baptism, without repentance, without reconciliation, without the restoration of his lawful and reasonable position as child of God, he dies as it were consolidated in that personal and independent world which he has made for himself by help of the means put at his disposal. Only after death the scene is changed. The body is gone, has done its work. The soul is naked. The veil which separated it from God is vanished, and the means of self-defence which the outer world gave him, the means of maintaining that state of separation and independence all alike are gone. The soul is now given over defenceless to the gaze of its Creator and its Judge who demands its account. "Render account of thy Stewardship," says the parable. Vainly would she strive to say "Give me a little time." *Time is no more.* Before the Face of God she enters on a state of things in which time as we know it here below is no more an element. She is in the position of a debtor, eternally insolvent; for the resources which she could use, on which she could draw while the world was at her disposal, fail her now. There is nothing now that lets her fulfil between Creator and creation her function of intermediary, Priest-Oblator. She no longer provides to God any communication with His work. She no longer is of any use to Him. Let her burn then, like that barren fig-tree which cumbereth the ground. Behold man, all alone, weighted with a debt which he can never more discharge, which God can never cease to claim. Let Him then, as the vulgar saying is in French "take it out of the beast"! He has placed himself in a state of finality. He hinders God. He will not let Him pass. He now has nothing behind him, nothing that can *back* him. "What hast thou done with that world which I gave thee? Give Me back what is Mine, of which I gave you stewardship for a time." Theology teaches us that Hell connotes two kinds of pain: the pain of *loss* and the pain of *sense;* what our Lord expresses by His similitude of "The worm that dieth not, and the fire which is not quenched." The loss is the *privation* of God. It is the creature reft of its essential end, incapable of satisfying that end, that profound need in his nature of belonging to God, of relating our particular and transitory being to His Eternal and Absolute Being: it is that unslaked need in the depth of us which our Lord designates as "Gnawing worm" or metaphysic hunger.

The pain of *sense* is the punishment of the actual sins

which are the consequences and the fruit of Original Sin. The right sense is that which goes from the inner to the outer, from the creature to its Creator. When we use our senses honorably and normally we do it to fulfil our needs as creatures, to discharge the task incumbent on us as servants of God, and as stewards of the good things He has entrusted to us. But when instead of seeking solely the service of God, the fulfilment of His law, which the Gospel calls " The Kingdom of God," we set ourselves to seek our pleasure or our personal advantage, we are guilty of a *contradiction;* we draw to ourselves, unruly and chance-covetous of their enjoyment, the objects of which our senses give us knowledge and desire, instead of referring them to God to Whom they belong. Thus we modify our moral organism. We turn it back upon ourselves. We make things serve an end, we make them move in a direction, which is not theirs—bent backwards, and there results for us in this life, morally, intellectually, and even physically, all manner of disorder, But when we die, we present to God a creature entirely oriented and worn smooth to its personal advantage, absolutely incapable of giving to God the straightforward service which evermore He exacts, of making normal use of the new surroundings into which it finds itself plunged. God bears upon her, and she can no longer bear upon her surroundings. Then she goes on fire within herself, and since God has made her indestructible, and moreover, *time is no more*, she burns everlastingly without being consumed. Instead of satisfying Love by the fire which makes it light, splendour, spirit, she satisfies justice by that same fire which without end questions, analyses, calcines her, strips her nature bare, shows her her vocation and her failure in the inexorable light of evidence. That is what the Prophet Ezekiel utters when he makes God say to the King of Tyre, meaning Satan: "I will cause to break out in the midst of thee a devouring fire."

This is all that my poor brain lets me say of these frightful mysteries, but how much easier it is to believe quite simply what our Lord tells us, and the truths which He puts straight into our mouths.

THE PHYSICS OF THE EUCHARIST

THE PHYSICS OF THE EUCHARIST

I. WHAT REMAINS AFTER THE CONSECRATION?

i. Firstly, of the Bread and Wine there remains something. What we see in the consecrated Host and in the Chalice forms one whole which has a real, concrete and objective existence. That whiteness, that taste, that liquidity are not an hallucination of our senses: they exist. They are appearances, but they are not illusions. Not only are these sensible qualities not altered, but neither is the relationship and proportion between them. Their position, their properties remain the same. They continue to react in the same way upon us and upon external things. What remains of the unleavened bread is still breakable and still nourishing: what remains of the wine stays transparent and could produce drunkenness. Both are corruptible; the signs have remained the same. Everything goes on in the bodily world as if nothing had been altered. Round about Jesus the veil remains unriven. It is the seamless garment.

For God respects His work and annihilates nothing of what He has made. "To no thing is He the cause of tending to non-being" (St. Augustine). These real appearances agree with our senses. Our body had to have its share and its perception of the Sacrament. It is under cover of them that the Redeemer willed to be not only present, but ardently desired. They are no longer true as signs of the substance which is God, but they remain as symbols. " My Flesh is meat *indeed*, My Blood is drink *indeed*."

How then could He take away from the appearances of Bread and Wine, even as He took them on, the power of nourishing and slaking? Not merely in truth but pre-eminently the Meat and the Drink *par excellence.*

ii. The name given to what is left of the bread and wine after the Consecration is that of *species* or *accidents.*

SPECIES (*speculum*, *speculari*).

That bunch of qualities which, appearing to our senses, helps us to recognise, to distinguish and to place an individual thing; the exterior form, the separate image, defined and as it were minted just as it is presented to the mirror, to the gaze and to the understanding. There are two sacramental species, that of the Bread and that of the Wine.

ACCIDENTS.

The accident is defined by the schoolmen as that of whose essence it is to exist in another (*ens cui debetur esse in alio*). It is the opposite of substance, which is defined " that of whose essence it is to exist in itself and not in another " (*ens cuius quidditati debetur non esse in alio*).

iii. Thus, everything absolutely and without any expenditure of what remains of the Bread and Wine after consecration, all that constitutes for ourselves the reality of these objective appearances, all that by which it is what it is to our senses, and which lets us recognise and define it, all that preserves uniquely the natural aptitude for existence in a subject without having actual inherence.

iv. Now, firstly, it is evident that what is expressed by the adjective could not be a substance; and that the Bread is not that whiteness, nor that smoothness, nor that taste on the tongue: none of these qualities separately exists by itself. Nothing can be used as its synonym. No more can the order or the proportion of these qualities among themselves: for they still lack that secret unity which ensures that all together they make bread; nor again any of the properties, powers and energies enclosed in this particle of matter, the property of feeding, of perishing, of being damp, pulverised, growing mouldy, of reacting in such or such a way to such or such external circumstances as our senses fail to enumerate. All that is not the Bread, for it is not all that which makes the Bread: it is the Bread which makes all that.

In like manner the quantity is not the Bread: the Bread does not change its nature whether it be a pound or an ounce. The dimensions are not the Bread: the wafer-disc does not change its nature with the variation of its diameters, and, since the extent is one of those things which remain after the Consecration, we must needs conclude that the extent also is an accident and not a substance, that is to say that it has no existence of itself, and the mode of existence which belongs to it naturally, is to exist in something else.

v. The consequences of this Truth of Faith are very important from the philosophical point of view. And what wonder that the Eucharist is the centre of our intellectual life, as it is the basis of our moral and religious life, as Bread is the basic aliment of our physical life? By the dogma of the Eucharist is revealed to us at the outset, contrary to what all modern philosophies since Descartes say, that extension has no proper existence outside the concrete quiddity which gives it root, support and origin, and that it is not at all either a substance, as Spinoza, Gassendi, and even Malebranche were not afraid to assert (*First Talk on Metaphysics*), nor a pre-existing form of the mind, as Kant prefers. In the second place it is especially because substance, the fundamental reality of anything whatever, escapes our senses (I do not at all say our knowledge and our conception, of which these last are the truthful intermediaries), and because all that by which it is present to our senses is nowise substance.

vi. This does not mean to say that beneath the accidents you must conceive some sort of abstract reality having no natural bond with them. The very definition of accident: "what naturally has to exist in a substance," is a clear indication that it is not naturally separable from the substance and could not be objectively in being apart, save by a miracle which baffles thought, since it touches the very springs of being. As the Catechism of the Council of Trent warns us: "We cannot find (of this change) any image or example in the alterations of nature, not even in creation." Still, without desiring to set up a comparison, one may remark that in other orders of reality the appearance and even the operation survive their groundwork. Thus it is, that by what the astronomers say, the star that is long since gone out may go on shining in our eyes and impressing the spectroscope and the photographic plate. Thus it is on another side that the bones or the garments of a saint, though separated from that soul, that person, whereon grace did rest, continue to do the deeds of salvation. The virtue which went out from the man united with God continues to go forth from his remains. I know that these comparisons sound thin.

II. WHAT IS CHANGED AFTER THE CONSECRATION?

i. What is changed after the Consecration is the *substance* of the bread and wine.

ii. Changed, and not annihilated, nor provisionally set apart. What was the substance of the bread and wine becomes Christ's substance, passes into It whole and entire without any waste. *Tota substantia panis transit in totum Corpus Christi* (St. Thomas).

iii. This conversion takes place the instant that the words of consecration are completely uttered. At once, under the veil of the species, time, as we measure it, ceases to be.

iv. Let us analyse this term " substance " of which I have repeated the definition higher up.

The word " substance " is made up of two words (so in Greek is Hypostasis : *sub* (what underlies) and *stare* (what stands by itself, what does not change form and position). It rėcalls twice over the root *se* (*esse*) in the double meaning : what is on its own, what is separated from the rest. And in the first place the substance is that which underlies. It can never therefore be what is above : it is not exterior, it does not touch us by the surface, it is not perceptible by our senses. In the second place it is what abides, what does not stir, what is identical with itself, what is one, what is common, what makes of several phenomena a simple being, what explains the rest and makes it possible, what gives it measure and proportion, what is the reason why, what is the resource and the necessary groundwork of qualities veraciously determined by our senses.

v. The substance is beneath the accidents, not only as maintaining them, but as producing them ; not only as giving them their order, putting them in gear, but as giving them being, since they could not even exist without it, and not only as colour and taste, but as such and such colour and taste.

vi. To produce (God alone creates) is to furnish forth that movement whose term constitutes the existence of the thing in our senses, and its way of existing as such. And the balance in lifeless bodies is attained once for all: they are the result of a process external to themselves.

But we see the plant spring and the animal, and we look on at this self-development by which they grow and maintain themselves. In the days of Genesis everything was called by its name, which has never ceased to resound, and of this its existence constitutes the clear echo. This name is an *order* calling up and calling out the means which admit of its attaining to its end, the sealed form which forbids it to go beyond. Nothing isolated, nothing without movement, and no movement without composition, and no composition without an anterior order and common intention. This intention in lifeless bodies is in its entirety imposed from without. Among living things it labours and grows internally with a freedom ever greater until at last in man, full consciousness attained, commandment is superposed on order.

vii. Coming to the end of our analysis, what we find under the substance itself is Will, the special intention of God Creating. "My words," says the Word, "are Spirit and Life." God speaks and the whole Universe replies. As the word is given back from the wall, each being finds in its end attained the means of gathering together all the elements of its reply. Clear answer to the Word which called it forth, and nevertheless the same: one in time in the *day*, the other in Eternity.

viii. What is a word to the ear, is an image to the sight. What is a reply is at the same time a symbol. We see the figure before the face is shown us. Metaphor and not participation around the composing unity. Natural things signify to us one of the attributes and the benefits of God. But the Sacrament produces for the soul what it signifies to the body. It becomes eminently true that water cleanses and oil penetrates and strengthens; yea, and that the bread and wine are at least meat and drink. But while water and oil increase their properties without changing their nature, the Host in the hands of the priest becomes the "Super-substantial Bread" and the real nourishment.

III. WHAT IS NEW AFTER THE CONSECRATION?

i. What is new beneath the species after the Consecration is our Lord Jesus Christ.

ii. It is of faith that beneath each group of Eucharistic Species Jesus Christ is present whole and entire, with His Body, His Blood, His Bones, His Nerves, His Dimensions, His Soul, His Divinity; but we must distinguish what of Jesus Christ exists under the appearances of Bread and Wine by virtue of the Sacrament, and what exists there *by concomitance.*

iii. What is brought about by virtue of the Sacrament (by the power of the sacramental words) is the conversion of the substance of Bread into that of the

Body of our Lord, and of the substance of the Wine into that of His Blood (*substantia in substantiam*).

iv. The living Flesh and the living Blood: Jesus Christ in the Eucharist cannot be divided. He is present whole and entire under each of the species. What is not present by virtue of the Sacrament is present *by concomitance*: that is to say, the accidents—the Blood with the Flesh, the Flesh with the Blood—and all that I have enumerated in § ii. Thus it is that for a deaf man a person is present whole and entire under the species of the hearing (comparison, of course, and not likeness). God under the appearances of the unleavened bread is an eatable God, and in the cup he is drinkable God.

When we communicate, we receive a substance which is both united by virtue of the Sacrament to the accidents of Bread and united by natural concomitance to the dimensions and all the accidents of the Sacred Body. Between these two worlds the Eucharist forms an indissoluble bond and common ground for both. In it we receive the substance of which one of the accidents is the quantity which Jesus unfolds in Heaven.

v. The Christ Who is to-day beneath the appearances is the Christ arrived at His fullness just as He actually is gloriously risen again, and seated on the Right Hand. No more the seed which is the suffering body, but the perfect Fruit which is the Body of Glory, "the first fruits of them that sleep," clear, agile, subtle, impassible.

vi. In this material world the Eucharist is the greatest of the Mysteries. To penetrate it, sense is of no use to us. Our Lord is so well hidden beneath the appearances that even His Mother's eye could not find Him out.

We have just seen accidents, that is, what by definition "cannot be save in another" existing without any substance. Now we have before us a real body like our own, really received by us and still independent of place and of dimension: hidden accidents, sensible qualities which nevertheless abide eternally withdrawn from any reach of our senses.

vii. However, let us note one thing: this Mystery which confounds our mind is accepted out of hand by our heart without reservation or hesitation like a simple easy thing, like a gift as supremely fitting as it is gratuitous. No better does our stomach relish the bread, than our heart, plunging forward in advance of our faltering reason, goes to the Eucharist not only without any doubt but with voracity and uncontrolled desire as towards a good which all our being covets. Nature uplifted above herself, as of her own accord and quite deaf to our arguments, speaks face to face with her Creator with a violence which disconcerts us. This is altogether the contrary of philosophic reasoning which goes on as it were outside us, and which the heart of hearts is so slow in accepting. In this case Being goes straight to Being.

viii. "After that," says the Catechism of the Council of Trent, "pastors may teach that:

" Our Lord Jesus Christ is not in this Sacrament as in a place. Things are not in place except in so much as they have some extent. Now when we say that Jesus Christ is in the Eucharist, we do not attend to the greater or less extension of His Body, but to His Substance considered apart from the extension. For the substance of the Bread is changed into the substance, and not into the quantity or the size, of the Body of Jesus Christ. Now no one doubts that a substance can be equally well enclosed in a little as in a great space. Thus the substance of air is as much in a little portion of air as in a great one; the nature or the substance of water is no less entire in a small vessel than in a big one. As the Body of Our Lord Jesus Christ replaces the substance of the bread in the Eucharist, one is bound to agree that He is in the Sacrament in the same manner as the substance of the bread was before the Consecration. Now the substance of the bread was as rightly and as entirely in the smallest part as in the whole."

ix. We must be very watchful of the meaning of this text. It is clear that the force of the comparison instituted does not rest upon a likening of the substance of bread taken in the vulgar sense to the Human Body of Our Lord. One is homogeneous and very like itself in all its parts: the other is a living and organic complex consisting of parts, of which each is what it is and serves the others only on condition of not being what they are themselves, although fully penetrated with something both individual and common. It is here a question of substance taken in the philosophic sense according as we have defined it higher up. The substance of Christ replaces that of the bread, but taking to Itself this way of manifestation to our senses. What makes the bread to be what it is, is present in each of these particles as well as in the whole. What makes the Body of Christ be what it is, is indivisibly present in each particle of the Host as well as in the whole.

x. " Our Lord," as we have read, " is not in the Sacrament as in a place." Enough to recall the explanations given in the first chapter of this Essay, to understand what the sacred magisterium enjoins us to believe on that score. The substance is the first reality: that which stands of itself, which exists in itself and upon itself. The accidents are what exist in another, and extension is one of these accidents. Therefore it is not the substance which exists in the extension; whatever be its dimensions, it is the extension that exists in the substance and receives from it all that it has of being. No more than the qualities, whiteness, perfume, etc., exist without a subject, do the qualities and dimensions (weight, volume, contour, etc.), which also are a kind of quality. The substance of Christ is present wherever the appearances are, and one may say even that relatively to us and accidentally It changes place when the Blessed Sacrament is moved about. But considered in Itself, It ceases not to exist uniquely and locally in that place in Heaven which allows of Its physically occupying that bodily extension of which It is the cause. When we communicate therefore, we receive under the accidents which are without support, the substance of the Flesh, and with the substance indivisible the whole God-Man Who is in Heaven. By this temporal Sacrament we are communicated, united with Christ in His eternal manner of existing. It is not He that changes place, it is the veil of this world opening, it is ourselves in Him who are in a sense withdrawn from time and place. Christ in the days of His human life gave us only His Hands or His Face, His Envelope,—and did not give us His Substance. The Eucharistic Christ withdraws His Hands and will no longer give us but His Heart and His Substance wherein is all the rest. On one single point towards Him the Envelope of Created Things has become practicable. The Body was too strong a barrier: it repulsed us as our like; now, as our like, it gathers us in, thanks to the frail species which bring Him to us under the form of assimilable food.

xi. As Christ is in us, so also are all His accidents, which are indissolubly united to Him: they are in us not according to the proper mode of the accident and the extension, but according to the proper mode of the substance which is their foundation and their cause. What union were more intimate? He wills to make us sharers in what is deepest down in Him, deeper than thought, deeper than the very heart. He makes us co-exist with Him, He makes us share His centre, His inmost life as Redeeming Christ in the very way in which He sets about making that Body which lets Him be Jesus Christ. His most Holy Body is in the substance which is in us as the effect in the cause. Not a throb of His Heart but our own can feel at the Well-Spring. The Eucharistic Christ is precisely the same who conversed with the Apostles, but they saw Him from without to within, and we entertain Him, so to speak, from within to without.

xii. One last comparison: In our memory, in our imagination, in our understanding, we can hold the most vast and complicated groupings. With the one word: "Paris," we make a whole town. Our mind fits in with every grandeur and brings forth its conceptions on what scale it likes, as is proved by the instance of the Sculptor, the Engineer, the Architect. Every greatness is in our mind according to the mode of the latter, not like the fish on a dish, but like the effect in its cause. What is true of the mind is truer still of substance, as regards those things which are made to exist in it. "You shall eat it up entirely," as it is written in the Book of Exodus. Entirely shall you put it away within. No longer for your eyes but for your nourishment, no longer for your curiosity but for your edification, no longer for your consideration but for your Faith: no longer for your instruction but for your construction. *The Christian another Christ.* Jesus, in order to teach us to make ourselves Christians and the sort of man who says: "I live now, not I, but Christ in me," addresses us wholly Body and Soul. He trusts us with His own key. He makes us do with Him as to our inmost life all that makes the Christ in Him: He makes us touch Him with a contact infinitely more delicate and complete than that of the Apostle's fingers when they went right into the gaping wound.

FIVE UNSUCCESSFUL LETTERS

FIVE UNSUCCESSFUL LETTERS

TO MADAME X

I

Dear Friend,

. . . .

Please note first of all that it is one thing to believe in God (or to feel gradually accustomed in practice to His presence) and quite another to be able to picture Him to yourself by the imagination. Every instant we are handling forces, electricity, for instance, whose nature escapes us.

A blind man hears a voice, he knows therefore that there is someone outside with whom he can converse. But he is perfectly incapable of imagining who this person is, where he is, and so on.

Let us go a step further. Let us take the law of equilibrium of bodies in a liquid. It is expressed by a formula. This has a real universal existence and yet we cannot represent it in itself, nor say where it is. It is incapable of realising itself in any place.

When we hear the third movement of the Choral Symphony, we hear someone speaking to us with a personality sundered from all matter and all location, and yet so strong that it possesses our whole soul, and we never think of asking *where* it is.

God is. That is one point. *Where* God is, is another quite different point. God has neither body nor matter. He cannot therefore be somewhere, limited as in a prison by something material. If He were in a place, then there would be another place wherein He is not. Now He is present everywhere.

When we wish to see a picture we make use of our eyes. When we listen to music we use our ears. When we think of God and meditate upon Him we do not need either our eyes or our ears, but a guide : our guide is the idea of *Cause*. It is as *Creative and Preserving Cause* that God is present everywhere. Everything is His doing and Himself abides ever Cause, and never effect.

You read every moment in books those feeble pronouncements about the world being so great that man is as though lost in it, that God does not notice his existence, and so on. In reality that is making God middling like ourselves. The true God is equally busy and just as careful with the setting up of a nebula and the organisation of an earth worm. With what incredible minuteness, what sympathy, what kindness, what wisdom, what compassion, what humour ! He keeps up a continual conversation with every being. He has made us. How then should He not care for us ?

The relationship of the effect and the cause are quite different : in the mineral which responds to God's interrogation by a numeric, geometric and unalterable form : in the plant and in the animal capable of self-motion, of development in a little cycle like a melodic phrase which makes up their acts of Faith and their thanksgiving: and last of all in man in whom the relation of cause to effect takes the conscious character of Sonship. "His eyelids," says the Psalm, "examine the sons of men." Where is the Father? He is enthroned at the root of everything. He is not in any place since He Himself is the cause of every place, of all the geometric and mathematic co-ordinances of space. Theology tells us that He is pure act, substance, self-existing. Our heart tells us simply that He has made us, that He mingles in our existence and our life as He is the Author of the idea of us in which we have appeared. And if you ask your soul where is its God, this simple ignorant creature answers like Magdalen: "He is there." She needs not to know anything else. God is not in reference to her: it is she that is in reference to God. Wherever God is, she is His and she is in Him. "Where I am," says our Lord in St. John, "I will that you also be with Me." And so let us not try to represent God to ourselves by imagination as outside us, let us try to meet Him within, through the heart, losing ourselves in His Holy Presence.

One can besides push further and penetrate even to the threshold of the august mysteries of the Blessed Trinity, but perhaps this is beside our purpose for the present.

II

Dear Friend,

I am afraid my explanation may have seemed to you too abstract and slightly discouraging. I think it would be clearer if I used a parable. Imagine two persons having deep need of each other: for instance father and son, a woman and her lover, a master and his disciple, separated by an insurmountable obstacle, but still contriving to communicate by certain signs which they interpret. That is the position of the soul and God. We cannot attain to God either by sense, or by imagination, or by rational speculation (still this last can give us the needful orientation). The one point at which we shall find Him is in the essential kinship which we have with Him, that is, in the fact that we are the work of His hands. It is in the work that we find the craftsman; it is in the self-consciousness which it puts on that the statue recognises its author; it is by creation that we recognise the Creator. It is by being fully sons that we fully know the Father. What neither sense, nor imagination, nor reason can show us, our own essence, the fact that there is in us a created being bound up continually with its Creator, explains to us. This is what St. Paul tells us when he says that there is a voice in us which cries out unceasingly "Abba! Father!" That is the voice which does not deceive, the vital instinct, strong as physiological obligation, in which we are not deceived. As the Psalm says: "The unrighteous have told me every kind of story, but nothing like Thy Law"—Thy Law: a word both very hard and very strong.

Such is the situation resulting from nature alone. But God by prodigious industry, and thanks to the perfect holiness, simplicity and innocence of one of His creatures has succeeded in crossing the barrier. This is what we read every day at Mass—" And the Word was made Flesh and dwelt amongst us." And the Apostle tells us the news with a great shout of triumphal joy which has startled every generation in succession. " What our eyes have seen, what our ears have heard, what our hands have handled " : God became man not to satisfy our idle curiosity, but to guide us practically and in all safety along the way of salvation.

Think well upon the image which I used at the beginning of this letter. Look upon your soul as a poor chrysalis, eyes closed, hands humbly crossed upon the breast, senses as though slumbering under the novice-veil of material things, but the heart awake, and the wings already fully formed on her shoulders awaiting the Resurrection Day !

" You ask me for an answer, but my answer is that question which is put in thy mouth by none other than myself."

III

The question of the Incarnation in the first ages of the Church furnished matter for three great heresies.

The first is that of the Patriarch Nestorius who denied the Blessed Virgin the title of Theotokos (Mother of God) and said that the person of Jesus Christ, the two natures, the Divine and the Human, remained completely separated, as for instance the body is from the vesture.

The second is that of the Patriarch Eutyches who, on the contrary, advanced that in Jesus Christ there was but a single nature, that of the Incarnate Word, and that from the Incarnation His human Body was essentially different from all other human bodies.

The orthodox theory is that in the Person of Christ there are two natures bound together by a substantial or hypostatic union, and that as our Creed says, He is at once true God and true Man. The human nature composed of body and soul is the mainstay which is informed, penetrated, maintained, illuminated, sealed, incited to movement and intelligence by the Divine Nature. The same Word which made Christ in the womb of the Blessed Virgin Mary goes on making Him apart from her.

Hence the Church condemned a third heresy, that of the Monophysites who acknowledged that there were in Jesus Christ two natures, but propounded that there was but one will (contrary to the prayer in the Garden of Olives—" Not my Will but Thine be done "): Pope Agatho defined that the will is a property of the nature, and that where there are two natures there must be two wills, but the human will determines itself always in Jesus Christ both freely and in conformity with the Divine Omnipotent Will.

Such explanations, which may be turned into a theme of endless reflection, and which have most wonderfully aided the study of the human soul, may appear somewhat subtle, but they form an indispensable completion to my little treatise on the Incarnation.

IV

ON THE INCARNATION[1]

God created all living beings to His own image. As He is Creator, He has made them creators. He has laid in the depths of their nature a special delegation of His virtue, of His power to call into being a creature like itself. As He is the Creative Word, it is not out of place to call this power a name or a noun,[2] since it is by uttering the name that you *call* anyone in the double sense of the word, that is, that you *sign* him, so as to distinguish him from all other beings, and that you *bring him on*. The Life Germ is therefore comparable to a word, an essential name, which calls to it all the elements proper to its realisation. It is the active and formative element, and that is why the philosophers give it the name of *form*.

This call does not sound in the void, and in the womb of another being like itself it finds the answer which it needed. As a note decks itself with its harmonics, as a colour calls up about itself all the dainty symphony of other colours which never again permit the gaze to lack them, something comes to nourish the form in wondrous wise, to realise and to analyse it, to answer by a wise dispensation and division, by a delightful humouring of each of its propositions. Behold a new name, a new being realising itself, answering *Adsum!* Here I am! to the call of God mercifully entrusted to one of His

[1] Written in snowy weather on the 34th floor of one of the highest towers of New York.

[2] Cf. *Ex.* xxx. 13 : Every man who is passing towards the noun.

creatures, complete with all its organs, giving it leave to exist as a separate entity, both as *common noun* (man, rose, fish, etc.) and as *proper noun.*

All this is done in the name of God and by virtue of a name in the likeness of the Word.

This mysterious name, as it gathers about it all the elements proper to its realisation, so in it we go on existing: as in it we have been created, so in it we remain faithful to our place as creatures. And that is what we call the *soul* in which all living creatures exist. The philosophers say therefore that the soul is the form of the body because it is therein that the formative power resides, the virtue by which every being is called forth and maintained in life as such. There is the *vegetable* soul of plants, the *sensitive* soul of animals, and lastly the *intelligible* soul of human beings. This distinction is based on the greater or lesser consciousness which each being has of its own part and of its own name, according as God has given it the power of uttering a transitory praise that passes away with it, or on the contrary of conceiving and of calling the Eternal.

Hence we remark parenthetically the supreme importance which the Church attaches to generation, since it is there that we resemble God and are associated with His creative power. Hence also it is that in this act we are forbidden to take ourselves and our pleasure as its end, as Adam did, which was the cause of Original Sin, in which we have all been created and go on creating other folk like ourselves marked with the same blemish.

After all these explanations, I have hardly anything

more to say to help you to understand the Incarnation. This very same creative power, delegated to each creature in His formative name, it has pleased the Word to exercise directly. In the Incarnation of the Son of God there is therefore no miracle in the sense of contradiction or infraction of the laws of nature; on the contrary, there is plenitude, the accomplishment in perfect reality of a thing which we see constantly about us realised in imperfection and in semblance. To the call of its God, to the questioning of the Word, human nature profoundly prepared and cleared of every obstacle and defilement, answered by the total gift of all its means; and from this complete consent, from this answer made by the creature to the Creator, came forth the God-Man, so " the Word was made Flesh and dwelt amongst us." The huge promiscuous stammer of all nature is at last finished and consummated in the articulation of a perfect name, that of its Author. The Son to name His Father took up all the resources of all created nature offered upon that pure altar, the womb of the stainless Virgin.

" In the beginning was the Word." In the beginning of every creature is a word which calls it forth.

" In the head of the book it is written of Me: then said I: Behold! I come!"

In other words, the title, the " headline," which sums up the whole work. May God bring all these words to bear fruit in your heart! I offer them to you for your Feast Day, the glorious Martyr, Saint Agnes, all crimson and radiant with her golden hair in the glowing blood she shed for the glory of Jesus Christ!

V

ON TRANSUBSTANTIATION

In my previous letters I have spoken about the existence and the nature of God, His encounter and His union with human nature.

We now come to a question of keener and more immediate interest for us: Was this union with God ever realised? And could it ever be realised at all, elsewhere than in the Person of Jesus Christ? Or indeed has He found a way of extending to all mankind the benefit of His Incarnation? This substantial union with the Father, has it remained peculiar to Himself, or has He found a way to extend it to the whole body of which He is the Head, according to His own promise: Where *I am*, I will that you also be together with Me?

The union of man with God is the aim of all the movement of Creation, and the consummation of this union is what we call religion or bond. By union I do not mean simply that of thought, of imagination, of sense, or soul. I mean the union of the whole man who is made up of body and soul. It had to be that in the person of man the whole material creation should be made capable of getting back to its Creator and of being one with Him. Hence the meaning of the sacrifices and holocausts of paganism and of the Old Law. It is not a matter of being like the gods, as was the perfidious counsel of the tempter, in other words, to make idols of ourselves: it is a matter of being *unto God*, of belonging to Him, and being one with Him, as the vine branch is with the stock, so that it may be said that they make only one (*unum sunt*), of *being informed* entirely by God, so that the word of the Psalm is fulfilled: "Ye are Gods," and so that in love, in knowledge, and free-will, we realise fully the word of Saint Paul which is worthy of long pondering: "In God we live and move and have our *being*."

Else what would have been the use of the Incarnation? Why should the Son of God clothe Himself with flesh? Why the flesh in Him, if it were not between His Being and ours a complete means of fusion and assimilation, between two natures cleaving together, but distinct?

It is not our soul alone, it is not our mind alone, which craves for God. It is our heart. It is our bowels. It is all our strength, active and passive, material and spiritual. It is all our *substance*. It demands of Him an avenue right up to Him.

This avenue is the Eucharist. At the Last Supper our Lord said, taking bread into His holy and venerable Hands: "Take ye and eat. This is My Body," and taking the Chalice: "Drink ye all of this. For this is My Blood. . . ." So the bread became His Body and the wine became His Blood.

What does all that mean? And what did happen? For neither the bread nor the wine changed form, changed shape, or colour or virtue. The senses ascertained absolutely nothing new: all that the senses can attain remains just what it was. What are called the species or accidents have not altered.

What is it that are called *species* or *accidents*?

Take the bread, for instance. The bread is white, but this whiteness is not the bread. It is the quality inhering. There is a certain consistency, but this consistency is not the bread. There is a certain taste, but it is not the taste that is its nature. It is simply a consequence of its nature. All this consistency, whiteness, nutritive virtue, are distinct qualities which are not special to the bread. *It is not they that make the bread, it is the bread that makes them*, unites them in a certain order and proportion. Beneath the bread there is that permanent idea which makes it be bread. It is the trysting-place which draws toward itself from every side the converging threads of the accidents.

And there is what is called the *substance*.

To use a grammatical term, the bread is a *noun* or a *substantive*, and all those qualities, whiteness, consistency, and the rest, are *adjectives*.

What then has happened after consecration, after our Lord's and, after Him, His Priest's—according to the invitation: " Do this in memory of Me "—pronouncing over the bread and wine the words which you have just heard?

It has happened that, by the most astounding miracle, and without the senses having any warning whatsoever, a substance has been replaced by another substance. What now draws the same threads of accidents which, united in a certain proportion, gave just now to the bread its outward appearance, is no longer what was beneath the bread, but what is beneath Christ: no longer what makes the bread be, but what makes Christ be in His Body and in His Soul, in His Flesh, His Blood, and His Limbs; but this activity is never more betrayed outwardly by any sign. It has adopted another envelope. Instead of being essentially visible, it has become essentially eatable. The noun, that creative *substantive*, by which every being is clad with the convocating virtue which the Father has given it, this name which calls and gathers about itself the qualities which give it communication and touch with all the rest, this name has altered without the qualities which it calls together being modified. Instead of obeying the bread, they obey Christ. It is no longer bread, it is the Body of Jesus Christ to which His Soul is indissolubly united. The substance of Jesus Christ is henceforward clothed with the appearance of bread.

Transubstantiation has come to pass.

Let us use an image which is not absolutely exact. What is it to define a thing or a person? It is to enumerate all the qualities in it which are accessible to our knowledge. What is it to name it? It is to choose a term which allows us to go either from these joint qualities to the person or thing, or from that person or thing to those joint qualities. When I name the *sun*, when my tongue forms the sounds, when my pen traces the letters forming the word *sun*, these sounds, these letters, in themselves indifferent, give to my intelligence, to my imagination and to my feeling possession of the sun. From outward it becomes inward. It fills with its light and heat my heart and mind. Well, what these material impressions, the curves and the strokes of letters all combined, what the qualities of sound and writing do for that heterogeneous and immensely superior reality which is the sun, the qualities of bread,—whiteness, consistency, taste, etc.—do for Jesus Christ. But they no longer communicate to us an image. They communicate to us a reality and give us communion with It. They no longer put us in possession of an image. They put us in touch with and in possession of a reality.

By the Will of God, after the Consecration it happens that the qualities of whiteness, consistency and taste, no longer serve to designate bread, to give us bread, to let the bread be possessed and assimilated, they serve to name Jesus Christ, to localise Him, to give Him, to let Him be possessed and swallowed down. In them He has made Himself givable. In them He has become accessible to our flesh.

ON THE TRACK OF GOD

ON THE TRACK OF GOD[1]

A great book ! A book fore-ordained to a long period of well-doing. What a thrill to be the first to have read it, handled it, to have stood by the fountain-head ; and how it redoubles the thrill when the author is our friend, when we have conversed at ease together ; and he is both ours by what was allotted to him of temporal and transient, and God's by what of Eternal has henceforth begun in him !

The idea we see constantly returning through every kind of hesitation, amendment and relapse, all through these leaves taken from a prison diary (a pathetic bundle which it is my duty to put before the reader), is that God and the religious truth of which He is the Source, are not fabrics of our mind, but that He is a Fact, a Person, a Reality, in some way external and concrete, presenting Himself to us, imposing Himself upon us with the Authority, the Mystery, the off-handness, the appearance, illogical and for us almost scandalous, of the creatures and phenomena of nature. A machine which we have put together ourselves, we can endlessly take to pieces and put together again. So it is with the philosophic fictions concocted in the train of Descartes by a series of famous theory-mongers. On paper it almost looks as if it would work. It bodies forth a kind

[1] Preface to *A la trace de Dieu*, by Jacques Rivière.

of symmetry both smooth-working and suspicious. But when we are set before a real Being, things are no longer so easy. Whether it be God or a tree, we canno exhaust it by our definition. The essential escapes us The sign is not identical with the thing signified, no even adequate at all. Not by virtue of anything expres sible in words does such a Being exist, or live, or be th cause of something else. Even as to a chemical body science has never done drawing up the list of it activities. It does nothing else than set booby-traps, o invent for it means of revelation hitherto unknown. A to the *datum*, natural or supernatural, the mind of ma has two resources. In the case of those verities whos evidence or reality is thrust upon him without hi intelligence being able to grasp them whole, or se through them, it can proceed by way of logical deduction This is done equally by science and scholastic philosophy which is a quasi-grammatical interpretation of the real Or else it can take its stand before this known-unknow in a state of freshness, good faith, candour, virginity absolute sincerity, as well as impassioned attention. I is the attitude proclaimed by Scripture recommendin us to seek, to sweep and clean the room to find th missing groat. To stretch out our hands if perchanc we may get to touch Him (*si forte attrectaverimus Eum*) It is this psychological investigation, fairly analogou (save the deep underlying sentiment of love and rever ence) to the dispositions of the Practitioner scrutinisin a phenomenon and of the Doctor or observer powerfull caught up into their subject, of which Jacques Rivièr ries to describe some processes. For instance, he will ubstitute for pure logical deduction (though not rejected nd though left in its place of eminence, and besides, no nstrument is one too many) a sort of description or opography. On this point the reader will note with vonder the pages of prodigious insight and penetration n which Rivière has spoken of the *localisation* of nysteries. So as to make myself clearer, I will use a parable.

There is probably not one of my readers who does not know that admirable novel of Jules Verne, *The Mysterious Island.* Some shipwrecked men are cast upon an unknown island where they believe themselves alone and abandoned to their own resources. Then at critical moments help comes to them from no one knows vhere. They find a fire lighted, a box of tools moulder-ng on the beach, a rope thrown from the top of a rock, enemies wiped out. None of these events but can be explained somehow, almost naturally, and the cursory ninds of the company are content to benefit by this occult collaboration without upsetting themselves to ook for the Author. But not so the engineer, Cyrus Smith. You see him in a thrilling woodcut, hanging, antern in hand at the end of a rope-ladder at the bottom of a well, scanning that black water out of which at certain moments he has thought he heard noises coming or suspicious movements (this is where, in reality, every evening Captain Nemo emerging from his submarine hermitage comes to stand himself the treat of the human voice). Then things go wrong and comes the dismal moment, dreaded by all novel readers, of the explanation, always so much inferior to our expectation.

The attitude of Rivière is analogous to that of Cyrus Smith. But the mystery surrounding us is altogether greater than that into which fell the five Robinsons of the Pacific in consequence of that balloon being torn by the tempest from its moorings in the square of a besieged city; and the signs which our apathy would like to get rid of are not so well put together as those few waifs on the sands, those ambiguous gestures which for a moment seemed to light up for us the impassive face of common day. No longer is it the case of a daydream, but of something well and truly formulated before us, in giant letters on the face of a mountain about a certain Absence proclaimed since the Creation of the World by the abiding affirmation of successive generations, affirmed, circumscribed, defined, inevitable, inescapable, undeniable. More than that, efficient and *administered* by a whole body of official intermediaries. Rivière is one of those sensitive minds set apart from time to time to rouse our attention to the amazing interest of so strange a situation. There is a wall. Rather than squabble for ever about its construction and the nature of the materials used, would it not be better worth while to try to climb it? And the very thing we are told is that there is a way of getting over. There is a way of pre-empting Death, and the hour is come at last to make use of the detailed instructions which we have received for the organisation of a personal enterprise.

But I see that my parable is getting us too far. Rivière

was not a mystic, not even a philosopher. As I sometimes said to him, and my remarks seemed to give him pleasure: through the basic honesty of his nature, by his itch for objectivity so to speak, he was above all a man of science. He had less the need of explanation than the relish of the fact, and his writings are full of analyses, whether it be of particular temperaments of or general phenomena, of a remarkable breadth and delicacy. He has the gentleness of great observers, their sympathy, their patience, their freedom from partisanship, their art of questioning, their being at home with the subject. But he has, too, the need of consultation and verification. He will never stop until he gets what he wants. It may be said that for him in a certain sense a thing is *true* as soon as it is complete; just as a horse exists when he has four feet and all the rest of his organs. What attracts him in the Christian Faith is its homogeneity with the real, made up of the same kind of evidence, of enigmas, of suggestions and quaintnesses, it is its sympathy with the event. You feel it settling down, that it is cut from the same cloth. Mysteries explain themselves less by themselves than by explaining all the rest, as a lamp is proved less by its wick than by its light.[1]

This is what Rivière wished to show in one of the chapters of his projected Apologia:

> "More interesting than to demonstrate the Christian Faith, would be to set out a temptation, to make folk fall into it, to describe it with plenty of detail, to show

[1] "It was first and foremost in order to understand, that I became a Christian." (*Carnets.*)

forth its wonderful cohesion with force enough tc make the unbeliever giddy, and leave nothing for hin but to plunge in."

Such an environment as he can never more escape— in a word the Catholic Religion must prove itself by a Catholic demonstration, that is to say *total ;* and by thi very totality it is true because it is Catholic, that is complete, because it is the key and the keystone of every- thing. It only overcomes by opposing every momen to every piecemeal criticism its indivisible bulk.

" Sympathy with the event."

In order to throw light on these words I think ther are some accents to be added to the otherwise admirabl theory which Rivière has set up of Providence anc prayer, developing as a whole the text of St. Paul : " Al things (for a Christian) work together unto good," anc St. Augustine adds : " even sins."

When one brings into court, even in summar samples, the enormous dossier embodying the questior of human liberty, one is struck by the following fact according as one rises in the scale of being (and I believ myself that a certain liberty is nowhere lacking, and tha its roots, were it only under the names of resistance anc inertia, are found entwined with the very foundations o nature) one notices that the causes or motives whicl make them supplant one another and act, are more anc more manifold and complicated. A stone submits witl relative passivity to laws on which physics and mathe- matics suffice to give us images rudimentarily accurate in the manner of those over-candid geometrics whicl children use for drawing: this oval is a fellow's belly; a rectangle, and you have a dog or a pig. According as beings become more distinct, we notice that they no longer "work" merely from behind, that they are drawn on from the front, as by a void which goes before: we notice that only needs and attractions remain ineluctable, and that a certain choice is left to the subject in responding to them by ways more and more varied amidst a crowd of aids and obstacles more and more numerous and shifting. A mollusc has only to face up to elementary problems, whereas the life of every meat-eater is a kind of personal romance.

Lastly, in the case of man, the situation has grown still more complicated, and the instinctive estimate of particular cases become indispensable to the simplest manœuvres of life. The organ of the general is the intelligence, and its instrument is liberty, which allows man to set in order and re-erect himself in the midst of that riot which surrounds him, and which has ceased to be a confused eddy and has become a current, a rhythm and a drama. He uses a self-governing activity in surroundings subject to more and more invariable laws which overlap up to that pure circle where mathematics reign alone. Man is free amid a world which is nothing of the kind. He has to harmonise his own movements with a multitude of movements having no dependence on him. He has under his feet amongst a crowd of companions a moving floor. He collaborates with a Providence which, like a great slope, drags down events, regulating the manner and the rhythm of their progress, but for the realisation of Its designs never dispensing with his willing intervention, and dealing with him by a delicate system of denials and challenges.[1]

It is easier to make out the efficacy of prayer and the part it plays, if we represent the event not as a bounden result of a series of mechanical operations, but as the trysting-place, in a point of the future, of many forces convened by the object, and endowed with different degrees of self-government; or rather as a result to be attained by various means, as a proposition in tune with the situation which pulls on our liberty with latent seduction.

It is only after they are fixed that the lines and the figure appear in due submission to the Geometry. A general sliding down, a flowing down a thousand channels round the whole perimeter of a basin, of the created waters towards their Eternal Well-Spring; the reply to an invitation whose name with minerals is weight, with animals instinct, and in the soul of man, enlightened by

[1] "I am sure that if anyone were to look at the events of his life as I do from the point of view of what was necessary to him he would see a guidance, a premeditation of every instant, which would show him the hand of God with startling clearness. But we see nothing because we always look on the side of happiness. It is captivating to see how each one's life is closely harmonised, how it is played, and in quicker and quicker tempo, more and more stringent, according as it draws nigh the end. In childhood there is slackness, there is nothing to pay, there is adventure; but, as one grows old, every blow tells: nothing more happens but what flings the soul at its destiny, packs it off, gets it on towards its own purpose." (*Carnets.*)

"You believe in Science because it gets together a great many facts. More rightly still must you believe in religion because it gathers them all." (*Ibid.*)

reason and Faith, true love. (*Amor meus pondus meum :* My love is my weight.—St. Augustine.)

The essential form of prayer is : " Thy Will be done."[1]

By prayer we share in the Will Divine, but also, as Rivière profoundly notes, the Will Divine weds ours.[2]

It comes home to us with its light and its efficacy. We leave off being a resistance to become a collaboration. There is a point in Creation where God is freely, willingly and consciously accepted. We conclude an agreement with what is best and consequently with what is best for us as well. By desiring good, we allow Him on this point to realise the best. We benefit by all the benign co-operations which our appeal to God, our direct movement towards God, permits us to fix around us and to canalise. We constitute the mighty kernel of a harmony: " as the Creator, so the Conductor " (St. Gregory) ; " as it were, the great Symphony of an Ineffable Composer " (St. Augustine). Prayer is the sovereign unfolding of our liberty, which binds itself by its most hidden filaments to the *tropisms* [3] of vegetables or insects and to the reactions of chemical bodies.

* * * *

Among the rough sketches of Jacques Rivière, though

[1] *Fiat voluntas tua :* " The fiat of Creation, sharing its omnipotence."

[2] " He asks us for a little of our weakness to soften His wills, to give them more daintiness, more fitness with detail. He borrows from us what He has no right to possess Himself among His qualities : partiality, preference for this or that, sentimental considerations. It is the meaning of those prayers which we feel that He claims, that He wants from us." (*The Christian Mentality Seen from Within.*)

[3] *Tropism :* Metabolism : assimilation and exchange.

it has been most deeply studied and stands out best from its surroundings, is the study to which he has given the name *Catholicism and Society*. Therein he unfolds ideas which to many folk will appear subversive, but which it was more needful to-day than ever to set forth. To oppose, let us say, rather than to pose, not as absolute truth, but as the necessary antithesis of a thesis in itself no less defective for being regretfully seen to take on with certain publicists the value of an incontestable principle and fact. What platitudes, what nauseating rigmaroles have we not had to swallow on the social value of Christianity, on the help it gives to established order and sacrosanct tradition. On the assuagement that it provides for employers and owners, on its natural alliance with constituted authority! With what incredible tone of condescension did they not consent to make room for it beside Auguste Comte, among the Caryatides called upon to support the throne of the Goddess Nation. For certain minds the social order is not an ill-carved joint, a precarious and feeble compromise of which the injustice is but too plain to see, but practically justified inasmuch as it serves God all the same by the peace, such as it is, which it brings to the greatest number, and by the humble facilities it affords to the only important business of salvation: conservation, the good of him who has, is for them the first principle, a thing so safe and beautiful that from it religion borrows the best brightness of its virtue and its truth. True it is that in this direction lies a road towards faith which is not completely inadmissible since it has proved tempting to certain freaks of the tribe of Ferdinand Brunetière, but there is hardly any road more disgusting.

In this Rivière remarks after many another, that the Church fits herself indifferently to every form of Government provided it leaves her the freedom to follow her Divine Vocation. But he cannot help putting his finger on a very significant fact: that is, that since her institution the Catholic Church has never ceased at every point of the globe and every instant of her duration to have difficulties with every form of society and of the State, even of those which seem to borrow from her their constituent principles. Whether it is the Roman Empire, the Byzantine Empire, the barbarian princes, the feudal chiefs or the Communists, or the most Christian Governments, or the Revolution, or the empire of Napoleon, or Louis Philippe, or Victor Emanuel, or the French Republic, or the Czars, or the Bolsheviks, or Protestant Sovereigns or Chinese or Indian, or Japanese, or Arabs, or Turks or Redskins, wild men of Africa and Oceania, there has always been something that did not " stay put " and has ended in disputes, persecutions and martyrdoms. One might say that it is the same thing for Society as for the individual, and that the idea of perfection is like a gnawing germ which never lets it rest. A bad description; let us rather say a leaven which never ceases working our inward idleness, a principle of movement, of acquisition, of architecture and of life, but also a principle of discontent. " The Kingdom of God is within us." It is obtained not as is thought by tyrants, system- and constitution-mongers, by overlaying inert materials or by ingenious juxtaposition of mechanical parts, but by a sort of continual *escapement* or of sacrifice done to the internal weight or tension. Christian societies are always somewhat in travail. We have to be continually coming to agreement with something that is alive. One need only compare the history of oriental societies, that monotonous series of rising and ruin, of dynasties exactly alike, with the *train* of Christian civilisation, to understand what I mean. Rivière then is not completely right in saying that the idea of revolution and progress is alien from the Christian spirit. These are simply words improper to express the fact of development defined by St. Augustine: "what was closed is open and what was hid is known." God's plan has to unfold.

It is therefore clearly inexact to say that there is in Christianity an anti-social principle. Rather should it be said that it contains an architectural principle so energetic and vast that no actual society is capable of harbouring and containing it completely, of providing our soul with that abiding habitation which it needs. And even that is not altogether true. Jacques Rivière does not ignore in the course of those pages which like these I have just penned (not affirmations but propositions) are the questions put to itself by a mind on the march towards the truth. On the contrary, he makes perfectly evident the profound principles of present social peace founded upon ideals like that of Brotherhood in a common Father, of communion at a single table, of acceptance for the present and watchfulness for the future, and of a general postponement of our personal satisfactions. No government will find Christians in revolt, but what is worse, it will find them profoundly indifferent. It feels a dull irritation on hearing that there is in a Christian soul something that does not belong to it, something which is not for it, and fundamentally escapes it.[1]

It feels that it is seen through, and that to the very depths of its provisory essence. It is not taken seriously. It feels that it is no longer truly sovereign but a kind of steward or procurator, an overseer of material interests whose services are accepted with a resignation which it is not always difficult to mistake for scorn. It works in an atmosphere of irony. Even beneath the provisory forms of state, those great natural principles on which societies rest, honour, family, country, property, religion does not accept without reserve or without control. She knows how easily they can go crazy: she says that she is greater and stronger than they, she denies their *a*

[1] "If there be a truth that must be borne in mind and that M. de Morny has just brought to mind with rightful insistence at the general council of Puy-du-Dôme, it is that nothing of importance can be legally done in France without the previous authorisation of the administration. If, as M. de Morny very well says, you cannot shift a stone or dig a well without the permit of the Administration, still less can you without this permit establish a miracle or start a pilgrimage. Whoever is busy with religious affairs knows perfectly that the Administrative Authority has not one way but ten, not one legal claim but twenty or thirty which make it omnipotent in these matters." (Prévost-Paradol in the *Journal des Débats*, September 3rd, 1858, on the Miracles of Lourdes.)

priori character, she believes that it is from God alone they derive their august character, and that no human relationship can prevail against His sacred bond uniting the creature to its Creator. When a similar idea has been insinuated into oriental societies, all built up on the despotic idea of the family, one understands how they shiver to their base. But the part of Christianity has always been to bring out beside her eternal freshness, her eternal newness, both the hoariest traditions and the most recent devices of the fashion as something outworn, deciduous, and artificial. The neighbourhood of Eternity is dangerous for the perishable, and that of the Universal for the particular. And as the faithful sing every Sunday before the "Sun": [1]

Et antiquum documentum
Novo cedat ritui.

That is the hidden principle of struggle, but also of renewal, which without their always knowing it is the medicine and the salve of Christian societies, and allows of their surviving their momentary forms.

Another point on which the thought of Rivière seems to me to call for explanation is when he speaks of the small relish Catholics have for "Reform" in the social domain. In reality they behave there as in the moral domain in which they always prefer a positive method to that of interdiction. The principle of Christian morality

[1] "Freshness floods the fainting story,
Shadows drown in living glory,
Sunburst does away with night."
(*Lauda Sion.*)

was laid down by St. Augustine when he promulgated his famous maxim: "Love, and do what you like." It is a case of planting a principle so powerfully as to seize upon and gradually imbue all the powers of the soul; like the leaven taking hold of the paste, it eliminates as it builds. And in like manner with regard to social abuses, to a direct opposition it prefers either a kind of undermining of pernicious passions or the development of institutions or virtues incompatible with disorder and drawing to themselves life and interest. It is, in one word, the application of the Apostle's recommendation: "Be not overcome by evil, but overcome evil by good."

Lastly, there is one point on which this time I am not at all in agreement with Rivière: when he attributes to Christians (understand well, I use this word everywhere as he does, as synonymous with Catholic) a resignation, a submission, an indifference to their rights, which history does not precisely show us. There is no Professor at the end of the Rue Soufflot who is not in a position to demonstrate to him, on the contrary, how much theology has sharpened and untrammelled the juridic sense. The idea dominating the Christian theory upon the question, is that of *stewardship*: the idea that in a man nothing, not even his body and soul, much less his family or his goods, belongs to him, that all is God's and for God, to Whom he will have to give an exact account. If all that belonged to him, he could show himself smooth and conciliatory. There are many more people than you think who by natural laziness would be prepared to forsake anything you like, but, precisely because nothing belongs to him, the Christian, when he has not made a general resignation beforehand into the hands of his Creator and received discharge, can yield nothing except for strong reasons and by a kind of dispensation. It is not a question of the convenience of the moment, it is a matter of eternal responsibility; that is why in the teeth of all socialistic theories the Christian is so attached to the whole matter of his civic rights, his goods, his children, his country.

It is not that he depends on all that: it is that all that depends on him. It is to himself and not to another that God has given charge of it all. He transfers to the domain of material interests, sanctified by their object, that inflexible obstinacy of which his Church throughout all the ages from St. Lawrence and St. Thomas to the martyrs of the Revolution, and from Innocent down to Pius, has never failed to give him inspiring example. Compare the abject servility [1] of the schismatic and Protestant Churches in the face of all their tyrants with the intrepidity of the great Popes and you will understand what should be the feelings of men who from their childhood have had similar lessons and have been brought up in this school of Christian liberty. The rest is Tolstoy.

I quite feel that my readers, when they have been through the book which I am endeavouring to open by

[1] A servility equalled only by their pitiful pusillanimity in the face of the most extravagant theories from Darwin down to Freud, provided they appear in the garb of the latest fashion. Contrarily to the precept of St. Paul's *Nolite conformari huic saeculo.*

this inadequate introduction, will come back to me with a kind of reproachfulness. Jacques Rivière—who was he? They would like me to undertake to explain him to them, and how in detail that work and that life accord. I cannot. Essential elements are lacking to me. I have always lived abroad at immense material distances from Rivière, whose face I have seen, whose voice I have heard but little. Our correspondence was frequent in the first years of his literary life, then growing useless it ceased. God alone, by Whom souls do thrive, knows the secret and the windings of those ways which are not our ways. All that I can say is that the life of Jacques Rivière seems to me one of those which cannot be explained by themselves alone, by the good or evil teaching which they show forth, because they are the type in which numberless others realise and inform themselves, because they have the value of a parable. It is the best illustration of that Providence Whose hand he constantly felt upon him, of that lowly, gentle, ever present, ever unexpected Providence, infinitely patient, ingenious, and artistic, of which he has spoken so well.

That it is which led this soul of good will through the pilgrimage of intelligence, from the confusion of adolescence up to that Christmas Day, 1913, when by an act in which noble deliberateness of judgment played more part than the exigencies of feeling, he fell upon his knees at the feet of the holy Curé of Clichy, the Abbé Daniel Fontaine, apostle of the rag-pickers and the last confessor of Huysmans. Forthwith war broke out, and that same Providence then it was which, far from books, far from the world, far from all his own, meted out to him in suffering and captivity that long retreat, that austere interview with God, that direct operation on the soul, by way of surgery much more than of medicine, that period of pressure and suppression, of pruning and purgation. When he came out of Germany, Jacques was ready. All his destiny for the eight years which followed was nothing more than making sure, a kind of overhauling as of a manuscript one sets out to read over one last time: a kind of testamentary verification of those things which deep down in himself he had already abandoned. He had not completely escaped death in 1914. He had simply been the object of a measure of postponement, and his military wallet bore the fatal fly-leaf. A few days of leave and respite until the individual calling-up of the 14th February, 1925.

"My God I thank you for all this joy" (*Carnets*).

TWO LETTERS TO ARTHUR FONTAINE

TWO LETTERS TO ARTHUR FONTAINE

I

Dear Sir,

Your letter reaches me at Tientsin, where I am now consul and administrator of a little town in the full swim of progress. It is a joy to me to be handling all these quite big and quite real things: tramways, sewers, electricity, and the ruthlessness of accounts.

You are right, work is one of the good things of life, and without it I do not quite know what would become of me at Tientsin. And yet I do not want to speak too badly of this country. It is not ugly—it is in some way not there. Three rushes and a handful of sand make up all nature, as in the tragedies an armchair is sufficient to indicate a palace. That suits not ill with a classic mind like mine! What holds the place of everything, is an everlasting sky, never veiled, cleaned like a window-pane with sand and vinegar, and so fleckless that it looks as if the eye could discern, one behind the other, the seven spheres of Ptolemy. It is splendidly cold, one breathes in whipped sunshine. The cold is what ties up everything, what reduces everything to its maximum of astriction and tension; what tunes the harp-strings. How full of stars the nights, and how one feels like approaching the mysterious moment of the solstice when the year finishes in great secrecy and turns again upon her round, and when the Divine Child was brought us by the Angels.

And to me also a child will soon be given. We expect it towards the middle of next month. What joy for me ! May he make up what has been wanting in his father's destiny. What mine would have been without this fatal taste for idle words !

I too am at the moment of great peace and poise of my existence. For how long I know not. I use it for writing odes, which interests me very much, and sets me free from the chatter of the drama, always slightly childish and conventional. Whereas there is Poetry in the pure state, only the movement and co-ordination of masses, as in a fine symphony. I have written one on *The Spirit and the Water*, and I have just begun a *Magnificat*.

The " Summary " which I have sent you is not an apologetic pamphlet, but a programme of themes for discussion, ranked in their logical and objective order. To give the Faith to anyone is an undertaking of another order, and I hardly believe that it is by dialectic process that you lose it or regain it. It is like losing the appetite. To get it back you do not need controversies, but a cure of which the active principle of infallible efficacy is prayer.

I am irked at the tone of resignation which I notice in your letter. Here is a man of sound judgment, right mind, and feeling heart. How then can he imagine that what is strongest, best, most life-giving in his nature, is what deceives him, and is to him a source of illusion and error ? Whereas the coarsest parts, passion, egoism, material instinct—those whose field is narrowest and can never go beyond their instrumental value without knocking straightway against death—that these are the sole certitude and the sole legitimate groundwork of our nature? There is a road. No! Faith in God, heroic belief in spite of all, in our salvation, are not a morbid illusion, a perversion of our sensibility, but the exercise and the martial proclamation of a generous nature, simple and sound.

It is the life in us that believes in life, and it is what dies that believes in death. What is the most in us is not the thing which is not at all. We must not slackly surrender our arms on the advance of doubt, but trample it intrepidly underfoot like ancient Job who knows that his Redeemer liveth.

When we contemplate the agitations of matter, we seek out their cause and object, and yet the soul of man is a document surely more delicate and more instructive an object of experience subjected to an observation many times more intimate and precise than all those instruments by which outside ourselves we are obliged to make up the insufficiency of our senses—the *Credo* of the Centurion, the "Rabboni" of Magdalen and the infinite grieving, the melting of her woman's heart, as she clasps the feet of her risen Saviour. Ah, it is not imagination speaking, it is the outbreak of the most human and the most terrible reality—it is being answering Being, and the creature its Creator. To who knows this prodigious explosion, all other feelings, called natural, will appear quite artificial and incomplete. This is what is found in the Christian religion alone and not in any other cult only by intolerable usage called "religion." I should need a great deal of paper to develop this idea: at least take the word of a man who knows all these "religions," not from books but by familiar and daily contact.

No, we have no duties except to others, and even towards them we do not get our obligations from them. Tenderly though they love us, and we them, they will leave us one day, they are escaping us even now every moment, and we escape them in our essential depth, in that profound solitude where God alone can penetrate, in that essential void which is made only by His absence.

There is the truth which broke upon me suddenly like a sunburst one Christmas Day at Notre Dame twenty years ago. There is nothing more real than Joy, there is nothing more alive than Life, we cannot do without God, and from Him to us there is a sure and trodden road. For it is the reasonable and natural Joy of a live being who finds his eternal order, already visibly and materially marked out in this world by the Church.

Tientsin, 1906.

II

Beloved Friend,

I have just received your letter which touches me deeply, almost even to tears. The feeling of having done good to a soul is the keenest joy a man of my age can experience. It will be sweet to me to think when I am on my deathbed that my books have not added to the awful mass of darkness, doubt, impurity, which scourges mankind, but that those who read them have found there the reasons for believing and hoping and rejoicing.

But to you, a soul so fair and noble, and so well formed to the truth, let me say—how can it be that you still stay afar off, seeing that things divine have such a strong attraction for you? If my *Magnificat* has moved you, it is, as you say, because it is the work not of a poet, but of a man annihilated before the Glory of God showing through those wretched lines. A man of your knowledge and experience must have left by the wayside all useless things and not taken with him any but those tried and solid things which help to live and die. How is it you have not reflected on that strange fact that Christians alone are the men who possess joy, and to whom their beliefs never bring deception, but on the contrary an attachment, an interest, and a wonder ever new? I have often heard Christians reproached with a small superior air, that the reason of their faith is the joy and consolation which it brings them. But it seems to me that we cannot find a better justification, because that is a *fact* and not a reasoning process. The proof of the bread is that it feeds. The proof of the wine is that it intoxicates. The proof of the breath is life, and the proof of life is that it makes alive! Those are substantial realities against which no argument has any purchase.

Many a time I have thought of you and longed to talk with you on this grave subject; who knows if the reasons which sunder you from the Faith are as invincible as you think? Arguments hardly change and, reading the first apologists, one sees that ages of error have not added much to the list. But the ignorance of things Christian is profound. I was reading latterly Parigot's book on Renan, and I saw there that the author was fully convinced that the great doctors of the Middle Ages pictured Heaven and Paradise as a dome where you could climb with a ladder and where the elect spent their time making music. Dante, who has wrongly been taken for a profound theologian, is to some extent answerable for these ridiculous notions. Doubtless neither Parigot nor Renan ever heard tell of the Deific Vision, of that knowledge which lets us know God by making us God ourselves, whilst leaving our personality distinct. But this sublime view is at the top of a mountain of reasonings which very few people have had the patience to follow, despite their incomparable interest. It is the profound thinkers of the Middle Ages who could take pity on our sentimental and disfigured dreams, our queer mediocre romances like those of Bergson, our absurd self-contradictory theories like Darwinism.

Many people are separated from the truth by a door which they think shut, because they obstinately try to pull it towards them, whereas they have only to push it. I shall never believe that Nature in her invariable and majestic order gives us lessons in anguish and despair. The believer quite naturally finds himself in harmony with her: not because he is subject to her, but on the contrary because she is subject to him.

One of the most saddening things of these days is to

see just men like you, born to be the heirlooms of mankind, rendered useless because they do not *believe*, because they are like greedy bankers who will not give credit. A man who is out of the Church soon becomes a man apart. He has nowhere to return to. He no longer knows where he is. He is stricken with that terrible curse of no longer being able to do good to anyone. He does not even know any longer what is good or evil. He cannot reply because he can no longer speak, no longer knowing what is yes and no. He has no more brethren. Men now for him are only effigies, shaken with meaningless movement void of sense and aim. All bonds are shattered except those with which he himself is strangling.

I thought of all that looking on at those pilgrimages of poor countryfolk which passed through Prague the other day, the Feast Day of St. John Nepomucene. I felt that I could have followed myself that old peasant who walked at the head carrying the Cross, mingled with those booted peasant-women who followed him with all their finery on their backs. Differences of country, of learning, of upbringing, are then like garments which have no great importance. It is the veritable brotherhood, not that of the Revolution but that of the blood and the heart enlivened by the same bread. There are no brethren save them that have a common Father. From world's end to world's end true Christians making the sign of the Cross understand each other in what is most essential to themselves. But a learned man does not understand a dunce and has nothing more to say to him.

They are no longer equal: one has nothing to receive from the other. It is the curse of Babel.

My new book will be based precisely on this idea of the beauty of the Faith, personal trust of man for man, of grace veritable and freely given, by contrast with the written law, with the dead, impersonal justice which the Revolution has brought back from the days of Tiberius and of Nero.

Excuse my speaking so freely, but everyone knows I am a fanatic, and I have nothing to lose. I reproach myself bitterly with letting poor Philippe die in the night, just when his letter to Gide showed me that he was very near conversion, if I had ventured to be a little less discreet with him.

Thanks for your good wishes, which I feel are so sincere. The three little birds are well and are my joy! My wife sends kind remembrances, and I take your hand with all my heart.[1]

[1] Arthur Fontaine died a Christian of most virile and serene faith.

WHAT THINKEST THOU OF CHRIST?

WHAT THINKEST THOU OF CHRIST?[1]

This is the question to which in every country of the world, in Japan as elsewhere, at any stage of the destined route, and especially when he walks it in full consciousness of his first steps, every educated man must needs reply. Suddenly Jesus Christ intervenes, and even those, the greatest number, who have gone by with a gesture of ignorance, discouragement, impatience, blasphemy, or rejection, sometimes ask themselves with a dim shudder if to the fundamental question which was put to them—personally put—there were no other answer to give; I mean precisely that which the Holy Spirit put in the mouth of Simon Peter on the road to Cæsarea Philippi when he made up his mind to abide for ever with Him Who passes not away.

"Thou art the Christ, the Son of the Living God!"

It is to help your countrymen, my dear Abbé Totsuka, to that blest answer that you have translated these luminous and convincing pages of our fine hand-book *Christus*. You do me the honour to ask me for a preface. I can only give you a testimony, not now one of those joyful acclamations of youth, but the reflections of a whitening head, which rests upon an everlasting surety.

[1] For the Abbé Totsuka as a preface for a Japanese translation of the book *Christus*, translated into English under the title of *The Life of the Church* (London, 1932).

I copy out for you these few pages from *A Holy Week Meditation.*

I have tried to look at Christ from outside in as rational and objective a manner as possible, using written documents much less than logic and monumental facts, if I may call them so, which history, bringing to light by a kind of geological labour, has lifted to an abiding significance, as incontestable as stone.

Looking to the picture given by the Gospels as only for the simplest representation, not contested by any—What is Jesus Christ? A Jewish Illuminate, who has left us nothing written, preaching for a few years and finally crucified by the Romans on the initiative and on the condemnation of the Jewish doctrinal authorities. To this obscure personality is attached the greatest religious movement which ever wrought upon mankind.

Let us start and go on from these data alone.

The first thing to notice is that the powerful intellectual and moral agitation of which Jesus was the origin did not in His lifetime eventuate in a material and political movement. There is no trace of a rising, of a rebellion, as later on that of Judas the Gaulonite or Bar Koceba.

The fact underlying the condemnation of Jesus has therefore had a purely doctrinal cause, and this cause must have been extremely grave, seeing the gravity of the condemnation and its execution by the Romans on the eve of the greatest festival of the year, and although public order was never compromised.

Another proof of that gravity is the hatred vowed by the Jews to the memory of Jesus (see Talmud). Just as the virtue, or, if you like, the virulence of His teaching was confirmed by the conversion a year after Calvary of Saint Paul, a Pharisee of the Pharisees. As it never was translated into any political movement, we must needs conclude that the teaching of Christ was related solely to the world of ideas, of conscience. It was something sundered from the temporal. It made a radical distinction between the world of material fact and the moral world.

On the other hand, it never posed as the destruction of the old religion, but as its explanation and development. Christ preaches everywhere in the synagogues from the official pulpits. Still the preaching of Jesus causes a fearful scandal among the authorities officially responsible for the interpretation and administration of religion. They thought themselves threatened both in their belief and in their official position, shaken to the foundations. One feels that the Pharisees are fighting for their lives: so not on the side of Jesus is there mere moral preaching like that of John the Baptist, but doctrine: doctrine pointed out by Him as the sequence and development of the ancient revelation, and yet scandalously new in the eyes of the detainers of the Law. Jesus must have said something frightful.

There is nothing more frightful than blasphemy. But precisely, we see that the deed laid to the charge of Christ is blasphemy, that is to say, an attack on the Godhead Itself. The attribution to the Divinity of a character degrading to His Majesty. What was that blasphemy? On this point we have the contemporary witness of Saint Paul. So long as there is an historic trace of a Christian, from the first conversion authentically ascertained, we see that that Christian believed Christ to be the Son of God, and, if he believed that Jesus was the Son of God, it is because Jesus had told him so Himself (against Renan). This affirmation was, in Jewish eyes, an unheard-of scandal, to them who at that period no longer durst pronounce the "Incommunicable Name."

In all the history of mankind, never has a religious revolutionary dared to proclaim himself the Son of God (God in the fullness and the meaning which the Jews gave Him), and that for very simple reasons: because he too clearly lacked both the moral perfection and the material power to bear out so great a title. Such an affirmation in the midst of the Jewish world was something unheard of, frightful!

So it was absolutely necessary that Jesus should justify this claim, that He should give striking marks at once of His wisdom and of His power; He had to bear witness of Himself, both by holiness and by miracles. This necessity was the greater, that whilst enlisting His disciples into a new way which set against them the whole official traditional authority of Judaism, He promised them nevertheless no material advantage, but on the contrary persecution.

Now the Man who alone of all created beings has ever dared to call Himself the Son of God, we see perish in the basest, cruellest, most humiliating conditions in the most complete abandonment. Is it not manifest that His doctrine could not remain under the stigma of such a painful defeat of its Author, of so complete a denial of His affirmations? For, different from other religions, it consisted less in a body of affirmations impressive in themselves than in the person of the Man who came to make them. Therefore there had to be a revenge. There had to be some sort of proof that this Man, who called Himself the Son of God, had not been overcome. As a matter of fact we do not see that the death of Christ was followed by any depression among His disciples. There was no interpretative explanation dragged in by the neck, no sophisticated taking of comfort. There were none of those bickerings, conflicts, schisms, which would have been the inevitable consequences of an untruth. On the contrary, the death of Christ appears forthwith as a dazzling and triumphant confirmation of His teaching. There reigns among His disciples a wholly new spirit, absolute unanimity of exhilaration, of overflowing joy, of unquenchable confidence, of enterprise in all directions. What was this new deed, this revenge which followed immediately on the catastrophe of Calvary? Saint Paul tells us that it was the Resurrection, the formidable miracle on which all Christianity hangs.

To sum up this exposition:—

(1) The doctrine of Jesus Christ engages His disciples in a terrible struggle with the old religion, which declares it heretical and blasphemous—and likewise that of the pagan religion of which it set up at once as a supplanter

and excluder. A Christian had not to expect treatment better than his chief.

(2) In the struggle they will be temporarily unarmed, without promise of a temporal triumph. Violent methods are forbidden them: they are sent out to conquer unarmed. A future of sacrifice, of persecution, and of punishment is set before them and promised.

(3) The Founder of the Religion, Who had called Himself the Son of God, dies crucified and disowned by all.

These are the conditions in which Christianity was founded. Does not common sense indicate that there must have been something in the other scale of the balance? Not only promises, but deeds? How else explain the "mad" (Acts) explosion of confidence, energy, and activity which follows the Crucifixion? At one stroke, in a few years, Apostolic activity fills the whole world. To engage people who are depicted to us as cowardly, inert, rude, in an enterprise which is represented to us as paradoxically blasphemous, void of all human hope, certainly could not have been an easy thing. Something must needs have happened. . . .

He that hath ears to hear, let him hear!

ON TURNING THE OTHER CHEEK

ON TURNING THE OTHER CHEEK

"If they strike you on the right cheek, turn also the eft!"

All the Passivists, all the Tolstoyans, all the fanatics, ave abused this text, wanting to raise it to a precept of bligation, universal and categorical. In reality, to be nderstood aright, it must be compared with other assages in the Gospel which have the same paradoxical, iolent, unrelenting character, a whip-lash stinging our nertia; assuredly Our Lord is not a boon moralist, "Bless-you-my-children" Joseph Prudhomme—a nealy-mouthed Confucius. For instance:

"The publicans and the harlots shall go in the Kingdom of God before you."

"It is easier for a camel to pass through the eye of a needle than for a rich man to enter into the Kingdom of God."

"Unless ye become as little children, you shall not enter into the Kingdom of Heaven."

"If anyone hate not his father and mother and wife and children . . . he cannot be My disciple."

"Let the dead bury their dead."

"Consider the lilies of the field: they toil not, neither do they spin."

nd even:

"This generation shall not pass till all things (the end of the world) be fulfilled."

All these divine outbursts must be taken as bearing on words elsewhere, and on facts with which they must of necessity be harmonised: for instance, soldiers in the Gospel are by no means warned off their calling. There are rich men among the Apostles and disciples. One of the Beatitudes says: "Blessed are the clean of heart." A parable not only recommends us to tear out an eye, but even forbids us to tear up the bad seed in a field. Another praises the zealous steward who sets himself to trade the talent he has received, and even the roguish man of business who makes use even to a bad end of his worldly experience. Jesus honours manual labour by His own example. Family affection is commended to us from the height of the Cross. Numerous passages tell us that the Day of Judgment will always be unknown: Our Lord in discussion often uses abuse and threat. With a scourge of cords he drives the merchants out of the temple; in His struggle with the Pharisees He does not turn the other cheek. He gets away by flight.

Thus we see that the texts on which the morality of the Gospel rests have not the rigour of juridical injunction. The teachings of Christ do not at all answer the criterion of Kant: "Always act so that the formula of your action can be raised to a universal maxim."

Quite the contrary. You might say that they take our twisting and diverse nature just as it is and limit themselves to making use of its every slant. All these counsels bear upon us not like general and precise commandments but like powerful instincts, obscure, spontaneous, unforeseen, formless, like physiological suggestions, almost like *temptations*. You might say that beneath barren reason, hard and trivial selfishness, a delicate hand came mysteriously to engraft a deep inarticulate force upon our soul, that wild sapling creature, who knows that in essence he exists for something other than himself, someone continually and slily intent on treason to our person and our interests; some nameless perfidy in us of love against justice. Our Lord spoke many words like seeds which sprout in due season, when the moment is ripe for them, at the term of a set of circumstances which bring them to maturity. He is like the careful husbandman who sets in his treasury *new things and old*, or like the physician who knows the use of such a remedy, or what is the function of such and such infirmity; that such a curative gland will not enter on its action save under such or such pathological attack. Life passes over us and at the desired moment provokes, to the detriment of our heathen nature, the explosion of these plugged-in cartridges. Nature goes on in us, but henceforward enriched and colonised by a super-nature reaching as deep as itself: by an irreducible garrison of counsels always ready to make sorties. The whole under the control and infallible magisterium of the Church.

For a hundred years the assertion of professors that Christianity is an oriental doctrine in the manner of Buddhism and Islamism, a school of resignation, fatalism and death, has been rubbed into us *ad nauseam*. It is unfortunate for them that the history of the Church from its origin down to our own days, shows us on the contrary a spectacle of intense energy, of universal enterprise, of spiritual, moral and material activity against evil and error which has never known decline, and which ceases as soon as heresy and schism have spread over a great part of her domain their death-dealing influence. To this our great minds reply with phrases about the "occidental temperament," the "pragmatism of Europe" which has been miraculously able to turn inside out like a rabbit-skin and change from black to white the negative doctrines of the East, and so on. It is Europe, it would seem, that by means of a mysterious "virtue" analogous to the *virtus dormitiva* of Molière, has made Christianity. I myself believe that Christianity made Europe. Indeed there is no need of much reading or reflection to become persuaded that the active attitude towards life, belief, and action, is of the very essence of Christianity.

When they ask Our Lord: "What is the Great Commandment?" He replies with the Scripture: "Thou shalt love the Lord Thy God with thy whole heart, with thy whole soul and with thy whole mind. And the second is like to this: Thou shalt love thy neighbour as thyself."

Since these faculties in us serve to love God and carry out His Will, therefore is it: firstly, that none of them is evil, that none of them is superfluous; that all the strength of our soul and of our body, of our nature and of our sensitiveness, is holy, precious, excellent, inasmuch as it allows us to do our essential duty; and thus it is:

secondly, that not only must we utilise them all, but even not leave any particle unused, not the least thought, not the least word, for we shall have to render account of all—stretch them out to the last extremity like the body of Jesus Christ upon the Cross, to the extreme end of our powers, and beyond. On this condition do we realise in very truth, each in his own way, the state of goodwill: *as thy strength so be thy daring*.

There is nothing further removed from Buddhist annihilation and Moslem fatalism. There is nothing in us incapable of ministering to our salvation. There is always something to be done.

It is false therefore to pretend that at any moment Christianity preached non-resistance to evil. He who would allow injury or wrong to be done before his eyes to one of his brethren to whom he is bound, without using every means, every strength available, to aid him, would fail the fundamental precept of our Faith. So too, with him who by the deed of an aggressor shall see diminished and impaired in his own person the God whose image he is and the neighbours whose resource he is.

The Christian's resignation, therefore, is not the evasion of the Buddhist who leaves in his enemy's hands only an empty sheath and a body without a soul; nor is it the blasphemy of the Moslem who says: "It was written," nor the utilitarian vileness of the Chinaman which is rendered by this maxim: "If a powerful man spit upon thee, wipe not away the spittle, lest he believe thee to be disgusted."

"Turn the other cheek," said Christ. It is an offensive movement full of danger and of menace, for we are stricken on the cheek, but we aim at the heart. It is a *counter-thrust*. By turning the other cheek we conform ourselves to God and of the insulter of a man we make the insulter of a God. So that now it is not us that this bully has stricken. He strikes at God, Who will unfailingly reply, the reply of His Justice, or rather, as we hope, of His Love.

MY "CHILDHOOD'S WINSOME FAITH"

MY "CHILDHOOD'S WINSOME FAITH"

Monsieur Souday was good enough the other day to devote to me one of his articles in the *Temps*.

The worthy critic has been visibly vexed in his convictions by the way in which I have allowed myself to manifest my own. Still he consents to excuse me by noting in his best bedside manner that, simple poet after all that I am, and chilled off by those "glaciers of the intelligence" where walk freely with smiling lips and quite at home, gay lads of the kidney of Ernest Havet and Rémy de Gourmont, I was fated to come back to "my childhood's winsome faith." Unbelief is a domain reserved for the heroes of thought; as for the others, they find a fit refuge in the legendary and flowery walks of semi-imbecility. What heroes at first-hand had I lamentably failed to recognise!

However, the remark of Monsieur Paul Souday deserves that we should dwell on it, precisely because of its great banality. In spite of all the phrases, a conversion is always a disquieting fact, and, to say the least, uncomfortable. The faith of a Catholic is not a matter of indifference. It is a direct and personal menace to the security of him who does not share it. For if, perchance, what Peter believes—and after all he is a man like me and has read the same books—if, perchance, it should turn out *true*, there would be consequences for Paul highly disagreeable to face. Therefore is it absolutely necessary to discover explanations for this phenomenon of faith, and above all of conversion. The simplest is that of a clouding-over of the intellectual faculties which suddenly makes the naïve take bladders for lanterns. As suddenly our own faculties by compensation receive a new brilliance, and this is flattering and fills the card.

In general it is the moment exact and triumphant where the quotation of Pascal's famous saying: "Quit your wit," comes handy. Monsieur Souday did not stop short in time.

And yet, if one were willing to look closely, with a mind free of prejudice, into things as they are, this evidence would at once emerge: that it is immensely easier not to believe than to believe. The world of sense surrounds us and presses on every side; it is simple to see nothing at all beyond. Powerful instincts impel us there is nothing easier than to obey them. M. Souday is an unbeliever, but the tripe-man at the corner and the dog-doctor opposite are the same, more fearless and impervious still. And if they all came out walking at the same hour, the glaciers of intelligence should be more crowded than the Foire du Trône.

A Catholic does not go walking on the glaciers. He lives in a world of hard realities, in which he finds himself bound to unceasing effort. What he thinks, what he believes, is not a greenhorn's fancy. He knows that life is at stake, and here and now. He is not looking at the Alps on a waiting-room poster: he knows that all he has before him is a kind of wall, sometimes very hard and very ugly, and that he must scale it or die. In less stately terms, he must absolutely put pressure on himself to subdue what is inferior in his nature to what is superior. He *lives according to principles*, which is the very definition of a rational life. These principles are not laid down by his personal whim ; that would deprive them of every authority and gravity, but by God Himself, of Whom it is not at all absurd to think that, being Creator, He is equally Law-Giver, and that, having gifted us with this great estate of existence, He can endow us with that still greater estate of a perfect existence where our ends shall come perfectly attained.

This Christian rational life is not at all easy. It is not easy from the practical point of view, and still less is it so for the convert who through his own fault has lost the benefit of habit and concentration which Pascal describes so badly in the word just quoted. The idea of losing one's independence of horse at grass, the obligation of periodically carrying to an authority, no matter how paternal, the most humiliating admissions, have nothing especially enchanting, and nature fights hard against these practices, of which reason alone gives us to understand the benefit.

In like manner to the intelligence and the imagination, the thought of being limited henceforth in their play, and of finding themselves locked into the pen set about them by faith, morality, and charity towards one's neighbour, has at first blush something fairly frightening. Only later on stand out the immense advantages which are the compensation of this wholesome discipline.

For the convert to pass over all these fearsome obstacles, and generally not without such hard striving that even the recollection is far from pleasant to call up, there must truly be something else than what so many folk imagine in the simplicity of their hearts: the organ, the incense, the stained glass, the Christmas Carols, Gounod's *Ave Maria*, the little sheep at the crib, and the lovely statues at St. Sulpice.[1]

Oh, it is strongly guarded against the convert, " his childhood's winsome faith." It has been easy for him to get out of it; it is a trifle harder to get back.

If the unbeliever, urged by that grace of God of which not vainly was it written that it is hard to resist, against all his inmost inclinations still makes up his mind to take the step, it is not because the Faith " is winsome " (what a word !). It is because he can no more do without it than without bread.

Later on, after long years, he may perhaps amuse himself with trying to reconstruct those very formidable objections, which an instinctive laziness disguised with the name of " reason " threw up to him, and hardly may he succeed. He will notice that these people who are so sure of themselves in their negations generally decline to discuss them, and, when they are asked what they believe and what they know themselves, are either dumb or incoherent.

He will thumb again those books in which once upon

[1] In a play I have just read a stout-hearted priest endeavours to revive the faith of a broken-down penitent by doling out to him these few words which he thinks certain to prove a cordial: " The cloister, my child ! The music ! The arches ! The *altar steps !* "

a time like so many others he went to look for " reason " and " science " and he will find them the most amusing collection of cock-and-bull stories, of begging the question, of contradictions in terms, of peevish and gratuitous assertions, of errors in fact, and of all the sophisms of which old Aristotle long since drew up the catalogue: not forgetting that most ingenuous and most frequent procedure, habitual with women and children, which consists in making illustrations do instead of proof. For it is quite remarkable, as in former days Père Gratry laid down, that there has never been worse reasoning than in this age when they talk so much of reason.

LETTER TO ALEXANDER CINGRIA

LETTER TO ALEXANDER CINGRIA

ON THE CAUSES OF THE DECADENCE OF SACRED ART

My dear Cingria,

I have already had occasion to tell you of the great value which I set on your book.[1]

I think it right from the first line to the last. I think it the most penetrating and complete account that I know on this distressing subject: the Causes of the Decadence of Sacred Art.

They may all be summed up in one. It is the divorce whose woful consummation the past century witnessed between the affirmations of the Faith and those powers of imagination and feeling which belong more eminently to the artist. On the one hand a certain religious school, chiefly in France, where the heresies of Quietism and Jansenism have dismally exaggerated its character, has in the religious act of adherence assigned too violently exclusive a rôle to the spirit stripped of flesh, whereas what has been baptised and is to rise again at the last day, is the whole man in the integral and indissoluble unity of his double nature. On the other hand, Art after the Council of Trent, generally known under the absurd name of Barroco, for which, as you know, I feel

[1] *La décadencé de l'Art sacré*, by Alexander Cingria. *Cahiers Vaudois*, Lausanne, 1918.

like yourself, the liveliest admiration, seems to have taken for its object not, like Gothic art, to *represent* the concrete facts and the historic truths of the Faith to the eyes of the multitude just like a great open Bible, but to *point out* with noise, with pomp and eloquence and often with the most moving pathos, a vacant space like a medallion, with its approaches barred to senses cast out with pomp and circumstance. There you see Saints whose face and attitude bespeak the ineffable and invisible: the whole disorderly plethora of ornament, with angels in a whirlpool of wings upholding a picture blurred and bewrayed with religious intensity, and statues that look as though they are blown about by a great wind coming from another world. But from before that, though of another world, the fancy shrinks intimidated, dispirited, and devotes all her resources to the disposal of a frame having for essential object to honour its content by quasi-official processes too soon degenerating into stale formulæ and pinchbeck glory.

But when, after the Revolution, the Church, fallen temporarily from her high estate, had to appeal to the artists for aid to restore her ruins, she found herself competing on even terms with the other customers who shared the market. Was not all that a brush contained then pledged to that undertaking which filled the whole nineteenth century: I mean that sort of general inventory of every show which history bequeathed or natural surroundings could provide, completed in our own day, methinks, with poor enough success? The religious crisis of the nineteenth century was not, maybe, a special crisis of the intelligence, for the arguments against the Faith have not sensibly increased either in number or intrinsic strength, nor in the learning of their champions; it was the crisis of an ill-nourished imagination, the senses turning away from that supernatural world where nothing happened to make it accessible or desirable. Great detriment to the Faith and greater still to the artist who, losing faith, lost hope as well, and, with hope, charity or the deep-seated appetite born of confidence in the absolute value of anything that may be attained or given. Hence there results a secret lesion even to the capacity of taking its object seriously, to the creator's essential mainspring which is the imagination or the desire of getting together at once for the benefit of himself and his neighbour with the aid of elements well-attuned, a certain image of a world at once delightful, significant and reasonable.

As for the Church, when she lost the integument of Art, she became in the last century like a man stripped of his clothes, in other words, when that sacred body made up of men at once believing and sinning, appeared for the first time materially to everyone's eyes in all its nakedness in a kind of showing up and permanent proclamation of its weaknesses and its wounds. For anyone with the hardihood to look at them, modern churches have the interest and the pathos of a long over-due confession. Their ugliness is the outward display of all our sins and faults, weakness, penury, timidity in faith and feeling, dryness of heart, distaste for the super-natural, tyranny of convention and formula, exaggeration of peculiar and unruly practice, worldliness ripe and rotten, greed, swagger, sulks, pharisaism, bombast. And yet within the soul abides, infinitely sorrowful, patient and hopeful, as one senses in all these poor old ladies wearing extravagant and lamentable hats at the prayers wherein I have made one these thirty years, at Low Mass in every chapel in the world. (For there is a negative poverty, but also a kind of positive poverty in the luxuriance of such unhappy flora !) Yes, even in those woe-begone churches, such as Notre Dame des Champs, like St. John the Evangelist at Paris, like the basilicas at Lourdes, more tragic to the seeing eye than the ruins of Rheims Cathedral : God is there, we can give ourselves to Him and He can give Himself to us that we may offer to Him still of our small personal means, for want of fitting thanks, a humiliation as great as that of Bethlehem.

Should we hope that in a world over which the banner of the Sacred Heart is soaring the misunderstanding which still exists between Art and Religion will finally pass away in the strong embrace of restored Catholic unity ? That Art, weary of imitating patterns for their own sake, will at last take a step towards the eternal world of cause and type, into the lap of a harmony once more heeded ? And that the Church in the person of her representatives will show less mistrust of those powers of imagination and feeling which form an indissoluble part of that humanity catholically redeemed not in one single faculty, but in all together, by the Blood of Christ ? Shall we admit that any of those resources of a world of which we have just minutely drawn up the inventory can remain estranged from the glory of the Redeemer? And should we believe that a material church will once more make seemly vesture for the Eternal Bride at home again in the olden honour and integrity of her hierarchic and liturgic institutions?

This is a thought which is not forbidden to us; this is that future, the coming of which books like yours serve to make perhaps less distant.

So be it!

Paris, 1919.

ON ART

ON ART

In Christian Art I see three periods : one *Hieratic*, one *Symbolic*, and finally a third which I shall call *Idealist*.

The first period, which embraces the whole of Byzantine Art, and which in the Orthodox Church has lasted right down to the present day, is directly concerned with the Sacred Mysteries, a conventional and liturgical Gallery laid down in canons rigid as the costume of the ministers and the sacramental gestures. Art is part of the ritual. Its object is not to evangelise and instruct, to excite our feelings, or directly to glorify God, but to set up about the Cross, about the Panagia and the Pantocrator, a crowd of official persons, a court, a choir, a clergy abiding on the walls, a pictorial outfit, the flat personnel of the Iconostasis, the embassy of angels and saints to which on Feast-Days the earthly crowd comes and joins itself. The Church is a *basilica :* that is to say, the Sovereign's residence amidst His court.

To the second period, which embraces the whole Art of the West from the sixth century to the Renaissance, I have given the name of *Symbolic*. The inspiring idea is that of a building that serves not only for the dwelling of the Godhead, but for our transactions with Him. A public square, a market-hall beneath its roof where the pillars frame and set the presence and the movement of the servers and the solemn duty incumbent, where the

Office goes out to meet the Sacraments, where the long procession of the days has come home at last and arranges itself in good order and ceremonial, spaced round about the choir. Not merely a pair of doves, like lowly Joseph, do we bring to the altar, but the offering of the whole exterior city in a display of relations and measures superposed and multiplied from every side around us. Since there is proportion, there is converse. All that sort of thing in the interior of the Church built on the foundations of the *Summa*—all that goes in, with all that lives there—is set on talking of God. In the solemn shadow of the Romanesque vaulting the low-brow workman, as he had not at his disposal woven fabrics pictures or mosaics, has quite simply supplied their place with the point of his knife on the jambs of the porch or the face of the lintel by designs, reliefs and gravings, the outcome of his own dreaming. Then came the words: watch him mixing his faith into the decoration and about the capitals, among every sort of ornamental and vegetable sally just where the upthrust engages the weight, he has intertwined sacred history with the twisting suggestions of the column, and meaning has invaded the whole building. There is conversation on every storey between the Church of long ago and that of to-day, between the Saints and the faithful, between the people and the Bible. Its episodes are played on this vertical stage, and the unlooked-for head, prompting or prying, here and there comes through the curtain of stone. The Senate, sitting numb in the liturgical gold of the Byzantine churches, has come to life. About the altar is no longer a mere constitutional presence, but truly a staff of ministers, an active presence alive and various, a manifold *representation* in the pictorial and scenic meaning of the word in the luxuriant detail of these intermingled scenes of the drama of our salvation. The Court Levée has become an Office, and, in order to keep it thriving, the whole repertory of our actual life, of nature and of seasons, of morality and of history, of shows and of ideas, amounts to a kind of holy riot, which takes possession of the walls, scales the steeples, and intervenes in every shaft of light, in the plans and the planes of the enormous Parable.

The third period is Apologetic and Mystical, a two-fold character which is fairly well summed up, if there is no fear of a pun, in the expression *Oratorical*. Baroque and classic eloquence does not less billow with draperies, does no less stiffen with porticos and colonnades, goes no less pompously out to the conquest of souls by the road of Prosopopeia, than the apostolic trumpet at the lips of a Bossuet or a Massillon plays rhetorical flourishes, groups into flattering perspective the battalions of its arguments, sweeps away in great surges its dumb-founded adversaries, irresistibly rises up step by step above the level plain of listening heads the many-coloured edifice of panegyric and of baldacchino. The sermons of the period look like set-pieces in golden pièce-montée which are plastic as pastry and sugar, and in them quotations from scripture are inlaid elegantly in fair Latin garlands like hieroglyph. The Church is no longer the *opus Dei*, the deed towards God of a collective worship, but an Opera seethed in incense, always rumbling with the thunder of an organ never more than half asleep; a perfectly lighted hall where the faithful come to the foot of the pulpit and of the Cross to receive Catechism lessons; a drill-hall in which devotion is gone through gymnastically for some time to the trumpet-tongued orders of a tireless instructor. The Church is superimposed on the social life rather than organically mingled. The cleric has withdrawn far from the layman. The Sanctuary has gone higher up and further away and does not connect with the man in the street save by a cascade of both contemptuous and favor-currying steps, like the consolidated mounting-step of a carriage. It is a permanent booth, an imposing protest of the spiritual against the brutal hubbub of the public square, a recruiting-station. And, within, the events and the truths of our Faith no longer constitute a part of the building: they have been brought there and stuck on, cut up into portable images. They can be taken under the arm and put anywhere according to their dimensions, whether it be a chapel or one's own room; they can be commercially edited, they can be put between the pages of one's prayer-book. And, just as the priest gives away to the children medals and good marks, he furnishes us from the top of the pulpit, or through the grating of his confessional, with private prayers, with personal tips for devotion and progress, indulgence-recipes, frameworks of meditations, the itinerary of a narrow path through the surrounding scandal which we are enjoined to look at as little as possible.

Understand well, it is not part of my intention to pass judgment on this modern atmosphere of piety to which the Church has had to suit herself in reply to the frightful Protestant depression. If it is up to the devil's expectations, how much more so to the Angels' too !

No doubt the time had come to make less room for outward forms and observances and more for free-will ; wills had to be put one by one on the testing block, allowing the inward gaze to take stock of ourselves in imitation of our Divine Model,[1] to wield about the inflexible and invincible axis of the Faith a supple strength of accommodation in reply to the crucifying propositions of a world enlarged, diversified and in commotion. All that I am trying to show here is the influence which this new conception of the tableau set by the Faith before our imagination has had upon the realisations of Art.

Stirring up souls to devotion has one programme, and praising God has quite another. In the second case it is Himself above all Whom we study to let speak, and the whole task of Art is to make Him better understood. The Cathedral is only a mighty apparatus for listening and replying, a prism in a sun-ray, an arrangement of echoes, a minute analysis and as it were an inward digestion by colour and relief of the Eternal Message. On the contrary, in order to win our hearts, you must woo our sensibility.[2] You must please. You must

[1] It is just the *Imitation of Christ* that opens this mystical and personal period of the Church.

[2] See Postscript.

encourage our heart in the way of Truth and action both by the overhead authority of bare dogma in the catechetic articulateness of the Tridentine declarations and by the taming of the senses. We must put holy dolls into the children's arms. We must fill their eyes with reality but with a reality at once abstract and seductive, the man of the philosophers and of the preachers. Something harmonious, soothing and eloquent, something catching, dare I say, something that will do its work all alone, something at the same time general and conventional enough not to refuse to any of our ideas and feelings the chance of catching on. It is the period of Art which I have called *Idealist*, whose principle is that we must give to sacred representation the maximum moral and spiritual winsomeness that painters can discover at the end of their brush, or sculptors of their chisel. Unfortunately that is little, for the surest way of finding beauty is not to seek it, and the Artist feels himself directly astray when he is told to keep an eye in his work on anything but God. From Murillo to Bouguereau, and to Mr. Luke Oliver Merson, the mere incline by itself drags us down from Raphael to the crystoleums which we know. The atmosphere is the same if the clientèle is different. It is not far from the Louvre to the Art School, nor from the Quai Malaquais to St. Sulpice, by a road paved with good intentions. And in order to bring back to modesty our populace with its ample loincloth and its flowing necktie, I will here introduce a quotation from St. Dionysius the Areopagite for which the involved considerations which are gone before have only served as a pretext.

St. Dionysius the Areopagite—he is represented with his own severed head in his hands, doubtless so as to suggest the subterfuge by which the real author of his writings, we are told, would have concealed his identity—in Chapter II., § 2, of his book on the Celestial Hierarchy, studies the question of what is seemly in the representation of Angels, or as he says " the shadowing forth of the Angelic names." It is surprising, he says, to see that in characterising them, Scripture takes its terms of comparison from amongst the brute beasts, bulls, lions, fowls of every kind. Would it not have been more seemly to choose from our vocabulary all that it has which is purest, noblest, most sublime, most spiritual? (Perhaps some will understand by this the abstractions of philosophical language—pale effigies with which we may quite well compare the wan idols and the twopenny-coloureds of the Rue Bonaparte.)

The Saint replies that there are two ways from the sign to the thing signified: one the way of likeness, and the other that of difference. God really, and the super-beings who are nearest to Him, infinitely surpasses all the ideas, notions, or figurations that we can make unto ourselves. It is less easy to describe Him by saying what He is than what He is not.

> " In things divine negations are true, affirmations are incongruous: to set forth unlikeness fits better the showing of their darkness. Things unlike them, if they do not add to their honour, at

least do not dishonour. *Si non condecorant, non dedecorant.*"

Thus the figures of the Lamb, the Lion, and the Fish for example, would more fittingly represent for us the Word Made Flesh than that portrait of a smart young fellow in a well-groomed beard. The disguise of a child, poor man or leper fits Him better than our tinsel gold-braid and that derisory purple cloak which mankind, since the days of the *Ecce Homo*, endeavours to put around His shoulders. He would have no other Crown than the Crown of Thorns, no other Royalty than what Pilate traced above His Head upon the Cross in Hebrew, Greek and Latin. It is when He opens His Heart to us on Calvary that He tries to tell us what made His Face dazzling upon Mount Tabor.

This text of St. Dionysius will therefore serve to refute those sour censors, those straitlaced Jansenists who take fright when they see certain artists treat the Sacred Mysteries with a familiarity wrongly deemed alien from respect or, as the ancient theologian has it, *saying what a shame it is to ascribe such ill-bred guise to most holy and Godlike adornments.*

As he makes him remark moreover a little further on, Creatures, whatsoever they be, are never unworthy of their Author by reason of contrariety but by reason of defect, seeing that He made them all in their kind and by the special word they have to say, *valde bona.*

Of course, it would be ridiculous to take St. Dionysius's idea too literally. It would bring us back to the worship of the beast, to the Golden Calf and all those brutal figures which India, Egypt, and the Fetishists have raised on a pedestal. The idea of St. Dionysius is that God is He Who exists, and that it is by everything which shares existence, by everything that is a substance and not merely quality, that we can best praise and apprehend Him. So it is not a question of improving on reality, working into a category by distinguishing what in it is more or less noble, but of considering it exclusively from the point of view of its constructional and expressive value. It is not a question of touching up, but of understanding and of grouping in order to understand. Anything that God has made, it is not ours to contemn nor cast away. *We have to comprehend.* We have to decipher on all creatures the signature of the Creator, the praise, of which he has made each the responsible depository, what it has to tell us of God, and therefore to read it from within (*intelligere*), to look at it without prejudice, with attention, patience, and sympathy, not in the attitude of a judge nor of a corporal, but in that of a brother, just as St. Francis spoke to Brother Fire and Brother Wolf. It is not a question of oiling and curling nature, but of setting her on fire. It is a question of coming to an understanding with her, and of explaining to her why she was made. It is a question in every creature of profiting by its essential difference, by what St. Dionysius calls its dissimilitude. It is a question of shutting out nothing, of gathering all together, of utilising the whole vocabulary at our disposal, of bringing the noun to the adjective, the verb to the predicate, and to the stalk the rich plumage of its fulfilment.

It is by taking our stand in front of Nature in an attitude of superior and disdainful criticism, by submitting her by authority of the Academy to our ridiculous theories, by cooking her according to the noble palate, which generally is only middle-class taste, by compelling her to play the harlot, by gainsaying and falsifying all that sacred candid word which her Author has put in her mouth, that from degradation to degradation we find ourselves surrounded by those sickening productions with which Italian marble-masons and patentee manufacturers have filled our poor churches.

And so it happens that in Art as in all other departments is once more justified the Gospel Word: "Seek ye first the Kingdom of God and His Justice and all these things shall be added unto you." But here I scruple, and a doubt occurs to me: all that infantry of St. Sulpice, all those soldiers of Christ whom their mothers made with flesh and blood, whom Grace re-made with fire and the Rue Bonaparte with butter, all those St. Josephs in cocoanut, and those standardised St. Teresas—how many fervent prayers have they not heard? How many simple pieties have they not charmed? How many solitudes have they not consoled? How many repentances and sacrifices have they not occasioned and witnessed? Of how many sacred intimacies have they not been the intermediaries? Of how many graces the instrument? Neither the Curé of Ars nor the Little Flower seems to have had a very distinguished æsthetic sense. The missionary who is going to get his nails and his scalp torn away for the Faith to-morrow, strains to his arms and waters with his blood a statue of the Sacred Heart, of which the best that may be said is that we should not care to have it in our best room. The Madonnas of Michael Angelo and of Raphael have never heard those delightful confidences which the Carmelite and the Little Sisters of the Poor entrust to a trade Virgin turned out of a sausage-mould! Are we to think that this impersonal statuary, if it does not slake devotion, at least does not hinder it, does not interpose between God and ourselves the irksome personality of the Artist? Must we believe that in their way they justified the deep thought of St. Dionysius, and that by their very ugliness, by their nameless ignominy, they are better fitted to speak to us of the Beauty inexpressible? Just where man—even a man of genius—takes up most room, there is less room for God. The castor-oil plant is indeed rather a miserable plant, but, failing the Tree of the Knowledge of Good and Evil, it has at least served with the impromptu pavilion of its broad pretentious leaves to protect the bald head of the prophet Jonah and purge that bitter man of his wrath against poor Nineveh! [1] [2]

[1] Not to mention that medicinal oil from which academic painters have doubtless pilfered the secret of their genius!

[2] I have heard good souls working themselves up because at Lisieux Saint Teresa has been dressed in white satin and coloured velvet-pile in imitation of the Carmelite serge. But the idea was no doubt to show so far as could be the transfiguration of our workaday integument. We had not the morning light at our command, but we had that velvet-pile and satin, which seem almost as wonderful to unstaled souls.

I am not defending the art of Lisieux, but often there, as in

These are ideas which his professional feelings make it very difficult for an artist to accept. He feels indignant and forlorn to see the whole creation to-day cut off from that word of love and thanksgiving which it owes to its Creator. He scans the horizon to see if the great tide of praise which he is waiting for is going at last to rise and surge towards the foot of the Altar. He asks all those workless and haggard loungers who loiter about the public square with the smile of the half-wit on their lips, why they do not join hands and march together towards the Mount of Vision. He knows all the difficulties awaiting the solitary man and the raw servitor. He knows that Beauty cannot be the reward of a chance inspiration, but the effect or the presage ?—of a general shifting of the horizon, a surge of the Universe, of a harking back to its foundations in the Work of the Six Days. *Bonum ex integra causa, malum ex quocumque defectu.* And since the movement of my ideas through the course of the present study is rather like that of the pendulum swaying alternately across the whole space between two opposing positions, the moment is come for me to pass from the point of view which I have just asked you to take up, dear reader, to another for which you will only have to make a turnabout: I will put it in this way: *The City of the Soul is built from above.* It is not the candle that

other holy places, beneath the imbecility of the execution, you unearth a poetic intention.

At Lisieux it is the Holy Face above the Altar that dominates everything, whereas Saint Teresa below effaces herself, and fades into the roses of childhood which she is scattering with both hands.

makes the flame; it is the flame that made the candle. It is not the Church which permits of prayer: it is the prayer offered under her roof that makes the Church, and passing from the world of spirit to that of matter, craves nourishment from regions which are becoming ever vaster and more profound. An evil action, an evil book, brings forth a surrounding wave of concentric consequences which reproduce themselves *ad infinitum.* But it must not be forgotten that it is even so with a good action, and with that operation, no matter how, at the end of an artist's fingers, which I shall call the work of glory. Amidst the curlings of a dreadful smoke and that biting sulphur which chokes breath and sight, it was enough that for an instant the gory gold of a desperate prayer lit up the poetry of poor Baudelaire making it stand out against the stream of opaque literature which accompanies and follows him, and showing that the "taint" itself was originally a gleam of faith escaped from the unseen world. The artistic impulse, a man's honest endeavour, when, no matter how, but of his best, with the means at his command, he tries not to parade himself but to *respond*, to answer a word by a word, a question by an act, and the Creator by a creation, cannot remain isolated, and it produces, whether its author knows or not, around him all manner of constructive consequences and propositions. This is indicated in Chapter XXXVIII. of *Ecclesiasticus*, where in a series of consoling verses the Wisdom of God deigns to lower Itself as far as poor artists, having drawn them away from their idolatrous practices, and Itself solemnly pronounces their justification before the Assembly of the Faithful.[1]

Even to-day in the nineteenth century, in this age of iron or, let us say rather, white metal, the Temple of Solomon and the Cathedral of Chartres have not exhausted all the possibilities of getting back to God. There is still something to draw upon from those folk with plaster in their hair and fingers full of paint. " Without them," says Wisdom, pushing forward, trotting out as upon a booth, all those poor devils, the Smith, the Architect, the Painter, the Potter and, what is most curious, the Die-sinker, the specialist in signatures, "without men of this kind the city will not be built." The city of bodies and the city of minds. The city of material and spiritual exchanges. A beautiful thing, whatsoever it be, cannot exist without fertilising all about it through admiration, challenge, contradiction, provocation, or through consequence. I mean a thing really alive, not a frigid, mechanical dummy, but something from which really virtue shall go forth. Saint Francis on fire brings Giotto in his wake, and Giotto brings the whole art of Italy. There are those whose arm is the trowel and the brush, and there are others who conjure up their building about them with no other instrument than echo. But a very curious thing: this city, which for very existence could never do without their collaboration, they themselves cannot inhabit. *Non inhabitabunt*, says our text, *non inambulabunt*, they shall not saunter to and fro like us busy men. And since they are to be neither citizens,

[1] *Labia deosculabitur qui recta respondet.* (*Prov.* xxiv. 26.)

nor vagrants, we may conclude that they shall have no proper specification beyond a kind of absence. *Non transilient in ecclesiam:* which I take the liberty of translating: "They shall not make a spring-board of politics": that is the province of *tumblers*. *In parabolis non invenientur.* When they lose themselves in explanations and theories, there shall be neither head nor tail of them. But behold their true vocation: *Creaturam ævi confirmabunt.* The passing thing, the creature of time, they shall consolidate. By giving it a meaning which time cannot exhaust, they will make it into something eternal. Their prayer is the working of their art. "Lending out their soul," giving their heart to all that they imitate, in brotherly and fatherly love, which will renew upon creatures the craftsmanship of the Creator. "And searching diligently in the law of the Most High," carrying on their exploration on every hand, of that vast realm which is the Law of the Most High, where "everything has been done in number, weight and measure," for we are reminded specifically a little higher up "in number is their craftsmanship!"[1]

Such are these diligent seekers after the Pearl of Price,[2] and the groat lost, or rather invested in the deep strongrooms of the Universe, whom the Gospel designates by the collective term "Scribes," that is to say producers of expression.

[1] *Assiduitas*, &c. (v. 28). In sustained attention is the secret of variety.

[2] The Black Pearl of the Tao.

The Kingdom of Heaven which they seek in the horizontal sense, will not, let us hope, be refused them in the other sense which is the better one.

So be it !

POSTSCRIPT

POSTSCRIPT

THE CHURCH IS A HOUSE OF PRAYER

On going over my manuscript I find lots of lines which cause the mind to hesitate, as happens every time one tries to apply the frame or the set mask of a scheme and system to the infinitely diverse and changing face of life. But the passage to which I should like to put the biggest question-mark is that in which it seems to be suggested that modern Churches are adapted to individual prayer : that could only be said of certain chapels. As for the Churches of the seventeenth and eighteenth centuries, I think I was right in asserting their " Oratory " character (which is found even in the emphatic prayers of our old prayer-books).

From the nineteenth century onwards, religious edifices in France take on a Concordatory character. They are buildings devoted to the administration of a public service: Marriages, Baptisms, First Communions, Catechism, Obsequies, Conferences, Works of Mercy :—in the case of the living, charity : or in that of the dead, the daily Mass for the intentions of the families X and Y.

The Sacristy of a Parish Church in Paris is as busy as the Municipal Office, and the temple itself is like its great waiting-room ; posters and print all over. Everywhere the noise of footsteps, conversations and the constant upsetting of furniture, not to mention the organist up above who would be very unhappy if he could not seize every occasion to finger his infernal utensil.

Where then should we go to pray? If we stay at home, we are in our own house and not in the House of God. If we go to the Church, we are most of the time as much threatened as Saint Anthony in his wooden hut, as he used to be represented in the village fairs:

> "Let's break them up, let's break them up,
> Saint Anthony and his hog!"

The Chapels are left: but to begin with these are not many. And then you are never sure of getting away from Canticles, vocal prayers, processions, the reciting of rosaries, devout whispering and chaffering, not to mention the service of the confessionals, which makes these blessed places not unlike a dentist's waiting-room. And, last of all, it is not easy for everyone to associate the presence of God with that glaring yet precious colour-scheme which gives the impression of an old maid in a circus-costume. Once you are in, willy-nilly, you are choked with lollipop, and oh! the smell of the furniture-polish!

Of course, I make allowances for all that is ridiculous and overdrawn in these wailings, and I leave to Monsieur Folantin the rôle of tearless grief and vexation which he sustains passing well. But, after all it is not Monsieur Folantin, it is Our Lord Himself Who said: "My

House is a House of Prayer" (*Matthew* xxi.; *Mark* xi.; *Luke* xix.).[1]

Since the Church is a house of prayer, what would you say, kind reader, if we were to try to make the container fit the contents a wee bit better, and the edifice correspond to its principal end? After all, we are not like Angels or Saints, ready to go into ecstasy, no matter where. For commonplace creatures, distracted, lazy, refractory or slow, finding it so hard to extricate themselves from the daily bog in which they flounder, external conditions have an importance which good sense and charity ought to take into account. Among the other prime needs of the human creature, prayer, which is the most essential of all, has this peculiarity, that with the majority of humans it is also the most hidden, the most ineffectual, the least sought after by the will, the least wrought-up by circumstances, and consequently the least liable to find self-expression,—deep down in us like a mortal ailment. Is it not therefore our duty to come to the rescue of this poor numb larva? When we see all the insects' wonderful precautions to bring on the unfolding of their breed, are we not aware that one of the duties of Christian Brotherhood[2] and of that most forgotten form of Charity which is Charity towards God Himself, should be the provision of surroundings

1 "I will rejoice them in the home of my prayer" (*Isaiah*).
"I have chosen this house that it may be a house of prayer" (*I. Macc.* iii. 46).

2 "With desolation is all the land made desolate because there is no one that considereth in the heart" (*Jer.* xii. 11).

where our soul, like a blissful worm, would have more chance to spin her silk and think out her wings?

So let us make an effort to settle modestly here some of the physical conditions of prayer and the material means which would be most apt to give them effect.

Of these conditions the first and most essential is silence: I mean silence of the eyes, the ears, and all the senses. When with good or less good grace the soul at last decides to take up her sentry-post, her first need is to blot out noise of every kind, that is, echoes, feelings, reminders, imagination, longings, all in stew and half-solution, or better still like that sort of dance of the cells which is called colloidal movement, in which she is soaked to saturation. One must also jerk the pulley-cord,[1] I mean, interrupt that automatic movement which unquenchedly brings images to the imagination.

It is therefore important to contrive about the subject, with the gentleness used towards neuropaths, a state of silence; and what is there in fact more helpless and more flayed-alive than the soul dumped down on the threshold of existence just like those premature infants which are put into an incubator? Interior noise is enough. At least let nothing from without come tearing and dragging and scratching and pinching and tickling and distracting the poor soul and bewraying her from the workings of that *delicate Sabbath* of which the prophet speaks.

[1] "Before the silver cord be broken, and the golden fillet shrink back, and the pitcher be crushed at the fountain and the wheel be broken on the cistern" (*Eccles*. xii. 6).

Either thick walls or its situation must put the edifice beyond reach of outer hubbub. Let us bear in mind the Temple of Solomon which excluded from its building the noise of axe and saw. We must abolish chairs and replace them by those solid and comfortable *pews* which exist in English and American Churches. We must avoid banging doors, rattling windows. We must lay down a floor not of stone or wood, but of one of those "felty" materials which the trade even now provides. It is fitting too that the Church be dark, so that our soul have fewer temptations to walk abroad.[1]

Or, if it is lightsome, let the daylight filling it not be that of the public square, but a clean atmosphere.

Last of all, the body of the suppliant ought to be placed in a comfortable and stable position. Kneeling is the attitude of prayer. Therefore it must be made easy by means of an appropriate piece of furniture. From this point of view, the common *prie-dieu* is a veritable miracle of uncouthness. It is good that the hips be sustained, that the arms find a broad support at the right height, that the knees on which the whole body rests be protected by cushions and that an ingenious collaboration bear up our bodies as the Angels are charged to comfort our spirit. Let us imitate the monks of the middle ages who constructed those strong stalls which seat you so beautifully and which place a misericorde under the back of the choir-brother. In a word, we must make it easy for the suppliant to forget

[1] Gold with gold commingling, shadow befriending shade. (M. Boileau Deschapelles, *Poésies sacrées*.)

his body completely. These are what I call the proximate dispositions.[1]

Let us now set about the remote dispositions which concern the building and its architect. When I was living in China and Japan, I often admired the plan of the temples which does not allow the believer to land straight before the idol or the entablature, but make him go round by all sorts of slopes and sidewalks, bridges, gates, galleries, stairways, openings, cuttings, screens, halls of secondary landings, so as to give the soul the time to pull itself together thanks to the preparations palmed upon the body. This is how in the Mosques we are invited to take off our shoes, in Japan to wash our mouth and hands in fresh and flowing water, and so on. The temple properly so-called is lapped about with enclosures and vast courts which cut it off from profane approach. You arrive at it by special and somehow spiritualised roadways. These are transitions contrived as erstwhile in Jerusalem from what is exterior to what is interior.

Not so is it with our modern Churches. In Italy the very street foaming through the ever-open door comes up to spatter the sanctuary steps, but in our old French Churches the preparation of the believer is replaced by a violent effect of contrast and surprise. When you go into Notre Dame, for instance, on a winter's afternoon,

[1] One might draw inspiration from the *prie-dieu* of the Emperor Charles IV. which I saw in Bohemia with the desk a semi-circle, so that one could give over the whole body to meditation. But solidity, stability, above all, are the essential conditions. *Juncti petræ.*

it is as though you suddenly dived into a bath of soothing darkness. What satisfaction to regain touch with our original nothingness ! The darkness in which we disappear renders us less remote from the unseen. Unfortunately, for various reasons, you will understand that it is not always possible so to serve up to the soul this magnificent helping of holy night, and the penitential delight of our baptismal tomb. There is always the dread, like a carnival cracker, like the raw-edged blare of a trumpet, of the explosion of those merciless lamps which have everywhere taken the place of the soothing and comfortable wax-flame. But like the engraver who sets out from absolute blank, the architect, whom here I am trying to encourage to exist, will have the task of qualifying the content of that holy vessel of which he has undertaken the shell, and to build no longer merely on steel and brick, but upon shadow itself, as essential material, and of feelings shaded and developed thereby, his system of solids. To-day, as on the first days of Creation, " the Light shineth in the darkness." Darkness is the very oil of the burning lamp and without its presence the lamp fails to attract our feeble eyes. Of yore this light we could but capture, make use of it as it stood, but to-day we are mighty to produce it, to send it gushing or oozing from the very substance of the building, to handle it like the most subtle instrument, to guide it like a spiritual attention applied in just perspective of various planes to an essential objective. The theatre, the cinema, the city lighting, provide us on the point with lessons by which it is surprising the Church has not yet profited. The ancient masons were not so timid, with their naïve endeavour to model the Madonna for the eyes of their children so as to bring down on her the brightness of an *oculus*.

To-day with how much more daintiness and detail may we not make alive, animate, underline, spiritualise even the mediocre work of a sculptor on the condition that it be not, as so often it is, an indifferent detail of the decoration, but a heartfelt need, look you, but the refuge, the life-buoy, to which the soul may come and cling, out of that night which has been vouchsafed to it for sojourn and from which this beaming orifice is its sole way out.

By means of night it must be given us to dwell in Light.

The problem is almost the same as that of mosaic. But, instead of light shining from the golden walls on to the interior of the building,[1] here it is from the very centre that it emanates, like the conscience awakening, the light itself grading the respective values of the thicknesses surrounding it, which is the material of our dwelling with God, and turning into colour at the touch of the members about us, and of the surfaces of the Ark in which we are laid away.

Here it is not the wall that makes the light, but the light that makes the wall. We do not inhabit a shape but a volume. No longer is it the space about us which sets us our point, it is ourselves that create space, and its

[1] Cf. III. *Kings* vi. 18. "All was covered with boards of cedar: and no stone could be seen in the walls at all."

shape is but the accepted limit where our field leaves off. We are afloat upon a kind of spiritual and liquid matter. Between God and us the distance is both filled and attenuated, impregnated with a virtue more subtle than incense. There is a conductory medium.

Of this atmospheric building, this life-giving bathing-pool, colour of course is an essential ingredient. Physiologists tell us that it has an appreciable effect upon our epidermis and our organs ; how should there not be also for our minds something below the infra-red and ultra-violet ? I am speaking of pure colour emancipated from the burden of reminding us of shows or telling us anecdotes, acting by its sole intrinsic virtue, something not only to be seen but to be breathed, something that is taken in at all the pores. How then should the engineer in spirituality whom I picture, not be interested in colour in general, in the tone underlying the arrangement which he has undertaken to bring about ? Pillars and walls : I see possibilities round me all red and pink ; others all white, with fine strong blacks, as at Siena. Others silver grey, with glint of glass and nickel here and there. Others all green, grass-green, banana-leaf green, and, laterally, a little ensanguined ikon of the Sacred Heart. Others like peacocks, green, blue, violet, and red, and great strong whites in others like beds of tulips : others intensely blue, like the sea at Cassis, like the pure and peaceful breathing of a flute ! [1]

It is a trysting-place for betrothals, the furnace of

[1] Plato, in his *Republic*, sees dark blue as the colour of his Purgatory.

passion, the cry of sacrifice ; it is the hall of studies, it is communion with the dayspring !

For our appointments with God why should not a washed-down pure spot be fittest, and what need have we of all those lustres and frames, those grilles and carpets, that overstocked bazaar about us, which only too well reminds us of the dreadful chaos in our heart and in our memory ? All those untidy spatters on the walls, those dismal catafalques, all that floundering mud and chocolate, and all those flabby histories droned on every side by fearsome sacristans ? Shall we for ever go on putting up with a tyranny of plaster and dirt ? And why should we not make use of all those materials—pure recipients of colour—which to-day are open to us : glass, pottery, lacquer, and the whole gamut of synthetic substances ? [1]

The eye which is the organ of sight, has also its own sense of touch, and it suffers amid barbaric disorder from the lack of contacts which might be soothing. If a vase seen from without is beautiful, why should it not also have an interior beauty, a hollow beauty, a concave gladness ? The important thing is to feel stripped—not to be trammelled by anything at all ; sticky, greasy, woolly, fuddled, bristly, stuffy, sulky, rude, which clings to us and deprives us of that free contact which the body radiates about itself. Give me what is at once gentle and hard, gold, iron, outlines and modellings which

[1] If gold is wanting, at least let its sheen, its lustre abide upon your walls, and all the dwelling appear unctuous with sacred unction like the stone at Bethel.

shall produce a feeling both of plenitude and of manifestation, of solitude and of company.

I do not want to be taken for a Mussulman or an iconoclast; I by no means exclude statues from the building of which I am here trying to discuss the imaginary structure. But imbued with the idea that the Church is a House of Prayer, to be at the service of prayer, I want the saints to assist us by their presence in figure as they have done by their presence in reality; in a word, I want statues to play an effective part, not to be an ornament, which is no business of ours, but of co-operation, the consolidated model in our eyes of their gesture towards God.

There are two kinds of presence: the presence facing us, people facing us whom we address, and a Presence beside us and behind us, unseen: all that whose existence we sense confusedly around us, the contact, the chorus and the pressure, all that behind us to which we are meant to lend expression.

It is plain that in the Catholic Church the middle and the place of honour must be kept for the Crucifix, which makes but one with the Blessed Sacrament triumphally elevated before the High Altar. If we consider the Church like a unique vessel and not like a street lined with counters, or a confederation of chapels, there is no longer any reason to change anything from the more and more widespread usage which keeps one of the lateral limbs for the Blessed Virgin and the other for Saint Joseph.[1]

[1] "Thy wife as a fruitful vine on the sides of thy house" (127th *Psalm*).

But the producer must take steps to see that what is put forward must be the meaning of the image and not its material side. We must not see all. It is enough that essential details show. For instance, that jewel in the Virgin's crown like a drop of heavenly dew; the Child's Hand blessing and in the shadow the august curve of the hip, or the rapt face of the patriarch built up and put together in the manner of indestructible joinery. Let the artist take inspiration from those dark holes above the Japanese altars where nothing is to be made out but a smouldering glow of lacquer and gold. Yet here is no question of a robber crouching at the bottom of his cave, but a living grace inviting and encouraging: not a shameless exposure to the garish daylight of our vulgarity. What is too much seen, and seen the whole time, soon ceases to be seen at all. In what we look upon there must be contrast and difference, a constructiveness which through the eye appeals to the understanding, and attention has to be prize of effort. There is now no longer any need for the same statue to be always in the niche; it can be replaced by another according to the liturgical occasion. Instead of the Virgin one could put from time to time one of the symbols of the litany, the Rose, the Gate, the Tower of Ivory. In our interview with the other life, it is possible to vary the elements of the dialogue.

"On the sides of the north, the city of the Great King" (47th *Psalm*).

"Thy sons . . . thy daughters, shall rise up at thy side" (*Isaiah* lx. 4).

"If his sides have not blessed me . . ." (*Job* xxxi. 20).

In front of us the sun, and at our back the forest. I mean that multiplicity and diversity which make up the outward world, now ordered, stylised, ranked, and arranged like the people on the Sunday, we must feel that we have it at our back, that we are its delegation, that we have with us the foremost ranks of an army, of which the rest beyond the gate becomes city, multitude —the whole creation.

It is like the Mass, where the general staff of pious women and devotees goes unhesitatingly into the first places to play the part of Cherubim and Seraphim, whilst as near as possible to the door the gross and groundling tribe of Gentiles, half-heathen, half-catechumen, is coughing and shuffling, stamping, sly, crooked, weary, cowed, awaiting with ponderous impatience the moment to get anywhere out of here, and betake itself away from this dubious atmosphere. Or, to use a more becoming comparison, it is as though the Saints like the Magi had come to Church, each followed by his folk and his flock, and had been halted as by a word of command at varying distances.

All this is perhaps a bit literary and ought to be discreetly interpreted, so as not to damage the feeling of unity and purity of the building, but yet how fail to see that in the model provided by God Himself there are degrees,[1] and from the portal to the altar a progress which ought to be marked by something, as, for instance,

[1] Compare the fifteen gradual psalms which make up the Little Office of the Blessed Virgin.

in Cathedrals at the foot of the Chancel that kind of lake formed by the transepts?

And how too should we not regret that, from that kind of miraculous draught taken by the latest century out of the ocean of reality, not one trophy, not one votive offering, has been brought in to hang from the vaults of our Cathedrals? All that, when we pray, takes part in the subconscious, wondrously sensitive and dainty, to which we are enrolled. For no one puts himself right with God without putting himself *ipso facto* right with all the rest. Offering himself, he offers all along with himself. When an orator is beginning to tell, he feels every movement in each individual of the listening crowd. So the suppliant ought to be as united with the holy place containing him as the chauffeur with his car. He senses the nation of the dead below his knees, and above him in the belfry all that bell-metal ready to moan. There is no need for a picture before our eyes, or the book for ever open that the effect be produced upon us. Their presence somewhere about is enough.

As to what I shall call the " service " or kitchen of the Church, parochial administration and all relations with the public, why not put them for ever in the crypt, keeping the Church itself as a place sacrosanct, set apart purely for the business of the soul with its God? Then it is that the believer can repeat in his turn, and even to the end of time, the prayer dedicatory of Solomon (III. *Kings* viii. 23):—

" Lord God of Israel, there is no God like Thee in heaven above, or on earth beneath: who keepest covenant and mercy with thy servants that have walked before thee with all their hearts. Who hast kept with thy servant David my father what thou hast promised him. Is it then to be thought that God should indeed dwell upon earth? For if heaven, and the heavens of heavens cannot contain thee, how much less this house which I have built? But have regard to the prayer of thy servant and to his supplications, O Lord my God. Hear the hymn and the prayer which thy servant prayeth before thee this day: That thy eyes may be open upon the house night and day [1] of which Thou hast said: My Name shall be there. That Thou mayest hearken to the prayer which Thy servant prayeth in this place to thee."

January, 1932.

[1] Why must all the churches be closed at night? How often has the wanderer groaned in front of those closed doors?

AN UNDERGROUND CHURCH

AN UNDERGROUND CHURCH

i. *Towns*, those places dedicated to the meeting, mixing and co-operation of crowds of men, are formed on the plan of a given region by the intersection of a certain number of axes, physical, political, economic and moral. But in the older countries history, caprice, every sort of contingency, constitute a factor of aberrancy, and as an instance we see capitals or seaports straggling towards a certain *optimum* point which they never quite reach. In America, where a large-scale map is immensely simpler and more readable, the compass without trouble plants a leg on those needed centres which by nature's will command the mighty net-works.

Among those capitals which have not only a subservient usefulness, a provincial rôle, but also a universal bearing, which are in a way the bases and the jumping-off points of Providence, Chicago is one of the most clearly designated. America is in essence, on the globe, a long vertical line from one pole to the other, perpendicular to the Eurasian axis. Between the two oceans it stands like a barrier, like a watershed distributing balance right and left. It is essentially a backbone. Of the two continental lenses placed inside this case, the Northern is the more important, and right in the middle of it a huge hand, like the paw of a monstrous animal, has left its print, the group of the Five Great Inland Lakes from which, one may say with in the main but slight violence to geographical accuracy, two great trenches give outlet —one towards the East and the other towards the South, the St. Lawrence and the Mississippi. Never was intention more strongly marked : impossible to write in more giant letters on the face of the earth : *There.*

ii. To this universal bearing of Chicago the magnificent Eucharistic Demonstrations of 1926, when by hundreds and thousands of representatives the twelve tribes of Catholic Israel came to adore the ever-present Saviour living and moving in the midst of His posterity, have recently called our attention.

Will they not leave on this predestined land an abiding trace, an *imprint?* Is there not something to be done? Our Lord has been uplifted for several days above the mightiest human gathering that ever contemplated Him. Will He not be asked to stay? Will not this great reservoir of humanity make room in its depths for Him Who loved men and had compassion on the multitude? Shall we not say to Him in return the words that long ago He spoke to Zaccheus: "Lord, come down!" "Our eyes," as the Psalmist says, "are tired with looking upwards." *Suspicientes in excelsum.* "Needs must Thou to-day make Thy sojourn with us. No longer above us, but in us, in the midst of us, we wish to have and possess Thee."

As the grain gathered from the ear is put into the ground, I propose that in memory of the manifestations of 1926 an Underground Church be constructed in Chicago.

iii. *Construct* is not the word that I should like to use. To-day the edifice is no longer a vertical pile of buildings pierced with openings and divided by partitions.

In reinforced concrete we command a kind of homogeneous material as obedient to our hands, as the clay to those of the potter. It is not now a matter of balancing a mass on foundations or piers. It is the modelling of a receptacle, a vessel. The Gothic Church was a kind of roofed-in forest, the altar in the middle of a glade overlooking a camp of pilgrims.

What I propose would be an organism, the most sacred of all, the Heart.

To this celestial grain, to this particle of wheat whose appearance hides the Incarnate Word, it is our business to make ready a tabernacle which may receive ourselves with Him. The Cross, which was to draw all to itself, has consummated its deed. The Church is no longer a meeting-place of roads, it is the deep centre where they all end. The Tabernacle hath swallowed the Church.

iv. All the Churches since Constantine have been raised with the idea both of illumination and of teaching. They are both beacons and pulpits ; the cresset set upon the mountain to be further seen, and the mountain itself. But to-day mankind is billowed like a flood, wave upon wave, and the Church is swallowed up in it as we see in the case of the poor "Trinity" in New York. One might say that it is all insheathed and incorporated into the crumb of the uniform human cake, like the honey-frames of the hive.

To-day the man who is seeking salvation, in vain would lift his eyes: let him rather trust to his own weight, to the mysterious force of gravitation which is the premier quality of his substance. *Amor pondus.*

Our wings are lacking, but we always have strength enough to fall.

v. Many Churches—and I do not speak of Italy where the sanctuary is so charmingly separated from the street by nothing but a half-lifted curtain—require an effort to enter. Often there is a long flight of stairs to climb, and, were it but one step, that is still too much for a foot heavy with custom and with sin.

The Church that I propose would on the contrary open under the feet of the passer-by like a trap. It would need an effort to keep from falling in. Its opening would burrow straight into the earth like the entries of the Tube or the Metro., or like those squints at New York through which they fling the coal into the cellars. There are enough churches already for the folk who have kept individual intelligence and will, things of which modern life, with the enormous collective pressure it exerts on soul and body, tends to deprive the dwellers in our urban deeps. They must have a trap opening beneath their feet, and nothing more for it than to run down in bulk like grain to the bottom of the silo, and there, suddenly, like him whom the tomb has swallowed up at a gulp, find the silence of God.

It is not a question of adoring God, but of homing Him.

vi. The First Catholic and Roman Church was the Colosseum, that meeting-place where all the roads of the Universe came to an end. There for two centuries in concentric circles sat all mankind, like a sort of tribunal or jury or court of enquiry, to ponder upon our fathers and mothers who in the teeth of the beasts bore witness to Jesus Christ.

The new Church also should resemble the Colosseum, or better, it should be a double colosseum, one above the other, a double dome, a double amphitheatre, each to other fitted and reciprocal, that of earth and that of Heaven. It should be exactly like the two valves of a shell (or again like the tortoise of Indian and Chinese mythology upholding the world). In the middle of the lower basin, Jesus Christ would take His place, and ten thousand men could kneel around Him sanctifying the modern idea of the Stadium. This Church would be always open ; night and day you could enter. Constant radiance always the same would reign there. Prayer would never cease, conformably with that text of the *Apocalypse* spoken on the day of dedication of a church : " And the gates thereof not be shut by day : for there shall be no night there."

vii. If you dig the earth you find water. The bottom of the sacred basin around which rank on rank the thirsty souls should throng, would therefore be taken up by a lake either of real water or artificial, meaning dim reflection. In the middle would rise the altar surmounted by the Monstrance.

This is not the place to insist on the mighty symbolism of Water, whose principal meaning is Heaven. The spirit brooding on the waters, the Flood, the water of Baptism, the waters of Salvation where dwells the mystic Fish (*Ichthys*), the well of Samaria, the pool of Bethesda, the brazen sea of Solomon's temple, the crystal, the semblance like to chrysolite which Isaiah and John described beneath the feet of the Ancient of Days. What more natural than to see Christ standing in the midst of the living water of the lake recalling that from which He so often taught and which His footsteps quieted, of that sacramental water which sunders and unites, that desirable water spoken of in the Psalm: " As the hart pants " ?

The whole heart's desire may always be reduced to the figure of the water in which every figure is mirrored. Guide we then our soul to this cup which is filled to the brim.

viii. In the middle of the altar like the stem of a stainless lily rises the Monstrance: it would well suit my fancy that the Altar and the Monstrance were of glass, that is, something like solidified water, like that cathedral described by the Irish sailor in the voyage of Saint Brendan.

So as to face the huge circle of the faithful on every

side, there would be four altars joined together like petals round the calyx, and the Monstrance topping the virgin shaft would expose equally four Hosts amid the rays of a four-fold Cross.

Four gangways stretching from the four corners of the Altar would link up with the shores of the sacred pool, so as to allow of Holy Communion being given. Between these four gangways four tribunes would support the lecterns where the Deacon proclaims the Gospel. At these four Altars four Masses would be said at a time, so that four Gospels would be read together.

ix. The upper shell fits the lower basin like a lid. It is entirely taken up in painting or mosaic with a gigantic image of a Byzantine Christ stretching out both arms, brooding over His people, and starred with ears of corn, vine-branches, bunches of grapes, adoring angels, and long phylacteries bearing great scriptural legends. The colours will be: red, blue, green, violet, white, black and gold. The whole rim of the shield to be taken up with a prophetic text, black on white. The colour of the dome to be reflected in the waters below.

If an alternative is preferred, the dome, instead of being uniform like a lid, could be deeply creased like those great scallop-shells which are aptly called holy water stoups.

x. For the lighting, I first thought of a peep-hole to let in a ray of light at a stated hour of the day. Without quite forsaking the idea, I fancy the slanting radiance of a powerful projector from below, striking the vault and so calling out in the pool a gorgeous perturbation of gold and jewel-work. A soft and gentle glow would constantly illumine the Sacramental Island and bring out here and there the glitter of a diamond or a tear. Someone, too, might fancy a sort of blue pervasion to fill all the praying hollow. By all means I consider that the Church has not yet made sufficient use of the resources of modern lighting.

xi. The Church I am describing would be altogether interior, so I have nothing to say about its external appearance. However, the concrete roof could be used for a winding Way of the Cross. But I would prefer all to be covered or hidden by buildings suited to the exterior works of mercy: schools, music-rooms, lending libraries, dispensaries, etc. Ventilation could easily be obtained by some mechanical contrivance.

xii. At first I had intended a great silence, unbroken silence, to reign over the great tank. No music, no singing. Still you cannot keep out of the place where the Blessed Sacrament abides Its own special ceremony of Benediction, nor that liturgy especially created by the Monstrance, that spiritual concert as it were, or, if I be pardoned the flippancy, that sort of serenade of a Sovereign by His court, the Motet. I am not an antiquary. I have deep admiration for Gregorian melody and Plain-Song, and personally I prefer them: they suffice me. But, if we ought to offer God all the resources of Art, why exclude those of Music? In speaking to God there is room for something else than the touching modulation of the naked voice. And as to what has happened since the Middle Ages, when you compare the depths of Christian dogma and feeling with the shallow sonorities which up to now have claimed to voice them, it will not be absurd to whisper that the domain of Sacred Music is almost virgin soil, and nearly everything is still to say.

Another notion is evidently feasible. Beneath the King's balcony there is plainly no objection to the concerted strains of an orchestra, nor to the wand of a conductor calling up the measured acclamations of a crowd. But in this pit which we endeavour to establish nowadays for the waifs and strays of a great city, in this species of set-pan for polluted waters, nothing must be allowed which would too directly gainsay the silence or refuse to blend with it. We will take our philharmonic displays elsewhere.

So I propose not to instal in this church, which ought to be understood as a tabernacle and a Holy of Holies, any organisation of music and singing, but to post it in a neighbouring hall communicating with the principal by openings more or less easy to blind, so that the music be less a positive presence, a profane activity, a disobliging actuality, than an emanation, the soul away down in blurred phrases telling God its recollections, its sorrows, its doubts, fears, hopes and sins, the whole life of man burning out somewhere in a hidden thurible like a murmurous elusive perfume. So the music, neighbouring God, communicating with Him, yet away from His immediate presence, dispensed from the stricter liturgical obligations and free, in this vestibule of the building and of the soul where it has been allowed to pitch its lecterns, to proceed to that examination of conscience, to those searchings of heart, to that clarifying of time, which are its most high duty, can set forth to Jesus Christ a lot of things which the poor creatures kneeling side by side around the inaccessible hollow have neither feeling nor words to tell Him. Gregorian melody is the Angels' speech, but music with its modern resources is a seemly translation of man's language for the ears of God.

The hall-annexe, being completely separable from the church proper, could be used for preaching and the various parochial functions.

xiii. There is now left but to speak of one of the essential functions of the Eucharistic Liturgy: the Procession. The King does not stay always on His throne: He comes down to His people, makes as though to be one with His Kingdom, shows Himself not only passively but actively. We must prepare for Him not only a Throne, but a Way, and the Eucharistic building ought to allow for both.

In a subterranean building this Way too shall be subterraneous. Before its lifting up in the ear, the celestial wheat takes growth and progress from below the ground, and the Catacombs come in train of the hidden home of Nazareth, the cave of Bethlehem, the

Arimathean's tomb. The first thing Christ's Soul does after leaving its divine Body is to go down to the lower regions: *descendit ad inferos.* The Church commences by the crypt, and even now there is going on a kind of preparation, plantation, consecration by the Founder Himself, of her eternal foundations. If the Cross is above, the stone is below. The work of Grace and Redemption takes in all nature, and before He crowns her summits He penetrates her depths.

This is why about the sacred hollow we contrive a gallery allowing our luminous entombed Sovereign, every week or every day, to go on a sort of symbolic inspection or blessing of the foundations of the enormous city of man piled above, and to draw an underground orbit around His proper mansion. He goes forth and a whole people follows Him, torch in hand. The walls of the gallery lit up by His footsteps are pure like salt and flash like crystal—frost-bound water, as one might say. Twelve dark mooring-rings, recalling Jerusalem's twelve gates, mark the halts of the procession. Here and there on the walls a train of crystals will wake memory of the colour of those gates, taken from the symbolic material of the stones of the Breastplate, as described in the Apocalypse. Immediately in front of the cortège, all is dark, but at the visible end of the gallery is contrived a flash-light blazing and quenching in the distance as God comes on, always keeping between Himself and itself the same symbolic interval in the blackness; that light forerunning Day and making ready the road for Truth.

Tokyo, 1926.

ECCE STO AD OSTIUM ET PULSO

ECCE STO AD OSTIUM ET PULSO[1]

Whilst I listen to the frightful storm which even now is shaking my whole house, I cannot help thinking of that verse of the *Apocalypse*: "BEHOLD I STAND AT THE DOOR AND KNOCK" (the Latin *pulso* also means "I PUSH"). What door is it save that disused door of our soul, that door signed with the Blood of the Lamb (*Exodus*), that mysterious Eastward Door spoken of by the prophet Ezechiel through which the Saviour of men alone is admitted! How sad and how unjust that this Door should be shut!

We are like a bad tenant kept through charity in a house which does not belong to him, which he neither built nor paid for, where he barricades himself and even for the nonce will not admit the lawful master. So then we are all alone on a night of tempest in our lonely and desolate house and suddenly there is a KNOCK! Oh not at the ordinary door, but at that old door which was thought to be CONDEMNED for ever, but there is no mistake, someone is knocking, someone has knocked! Someone has knocked at us and it has hurt us, like the child for the first time stirring in his mother.

Who has knocked? There is no mistake, it is He Who comes like a thief in the night, He of Whom it is written: "Behold the Bridegroom cometh, go ye forth

[1] From a letter.

to meet Him!" And we listen, throbbing. Perhaps He will knock but once. Perchance He will batter the door all night, as at times we hear until the morning that maddening shutter which keeps on rattling and flapping. But it is such a bore to get up and open that old door! It is fastened with two bolts, making but one of what is mobile and what is inert: one is called *bad habit* and the other *bad will.* As for the lock, that is our own secret. The key is lost. We must have oil to make it work. Besides what would happen if one opened the door? Night, the great wind of the prime breathing on the Waters, someone that we do not see but who will never again leave us in comfort by our own fireside. Spirit of God, keep out! I am afraid of draughts!

However, there is a knock. And how have we been knocked? In our affection, in our fortune, in our flesh. God does not knock merely, HE PUSHES. Sometimes a violent push, a thorough test of our resistance, sometimes an insistent pressure, teasing continuous. Not merely does He push, He beats (*pulso*, pulsation), like the arteries—an ache about a gaping wound. HE TOUCHES with one of those sudden touches which stop the heart. Or simply He mingles with every beat of that heart which He has made, which ever goes on making us, of that forge within us which goes on striking out sensation and idea. He unceasingly assaults and ever, everywhere, He only meets that hard unmoving party-wall. Ah, Lord, we will try to open unto You, we know it hurts You to keep knocking at us. . . .

Chuzenji, 1922.

TWO LETTERS ABOUT ST. JOSEPH

TWO LETTERS ABOUT ST. JOSEPH

TO SYLVANUS PITT

I

Dear Friend,

You ask me to talk to you from time to time and tell you what my mind is full of. Well, what fills it at the moment is that great and rather mysterious figure, St. Joseph, whose very name provokes a smile from superior persons. He was at once a workman and a gentleman. He was cheerful and silent, with a big noble nose, muscular arms and hands, with one finger often wrapped in rag, as is the way with those who labour in wood. He was not popular with Nazareth folk—they scarcely are who follow a peculiar calling.

And what more singular for a man than virginity, especially at that period? Why had he taken it on himself? How patient he must have been and strong against boredom, like the sun beginning the same round every morning without weariness.

I see him on an autumn day coming back from Caïffa where he went to fetch timber in a broken-down cart. I see him crossing the Sizon at the spot where the plain of Esdraelon unfolds before you, up to the trans-Jordanian mountains, the territory of six of the tribes. The cart sinks to its axles in the mud.

Then I see him in his workshop on a sunny morning.

I hear the saw and the hollow noise of balks of timber, and a child coming to look for him and calling " Joseph, Joseph " (perhaps that has some bearing one way or another on his departure for Jerusalem). His workshop must have been dear to children, as joiners' workshops always are.

Next I see him coming back from Jerusalem with his Bride so young and gentle (not much more than he beloved by the townfolk) I see them landing at home, and the obliging neighbour who had been getting the household ready ; the remarks about it all at the well in the evening.

Joseph is the patron of the hidden life, Scripture does not report a single word of his, it is the silence who is Father to the Word. What contrasts are in him ! He is the patron of bachelors and of fathers of family, of laymen and contemplatives, of priests and of business men ! For Joseph was a carpenter. He had to argue with customers and sign small contracts ; to follow up bad debts, to plead, to compromise, to buy his goods cheapest while ruminating on the second-hand, and so on.

How his last days of failing health must have been touching between Jesus and Mary, when he could no longer work ! I see the coachman of one of those fine ladies who went to the waters at Tiberias drawing up at the sick carpenter's to get the carriage mended. Jesus Himself takes it over and takes the tools from his hands.

All this goes on without a word when the Roman Empire, was at its zenith, full of pride and crime like our present civilisation. It is neither Cæsar nor Plato. Here are only three poor folk loving one another, and they are going to change the face of the world. It all goes on at the foot of a round mountain called Tabor; and in the distance is seen the long summit of Carmel. The villages near by are called Cana, Nahum, Endor, Mageddo. In three hours you get that brilliant country round the Lake of Genezareth which was then what Aix les Bains is to-day, but now lonely and unpeopled ![1]

Prague, 1922.

II

Dear Friend,

I want to unfold a few new ideas on St. Joseph, as your friendly questioning revealed their presence the other day in a dim corner of my mind, where they have ever since been queerly slumbering. But to develop the idea logically, to bring the conclusion pleasantly out of the premiss like the joints of a telescope, is something I do not feel up to every day. My own mind is so geared that at times it works by sudden leaps and bounds. The reader has to get on friendly terms with the stray rabbit that knocks up against the furniture, to watch the right moment to catch him by the paw or by the ears before restoring him to the conjuror's hat! Or if you

[1] As to what was made in the workshops at Nazareth, Father Schwelm has given some likely details: "Orders may be pictured in accordance with the known business of the Joiner-Carpenter among the Jews; beams to be squared for the support of the terraces which crowned the houses; harness-shafts and goads for the tillers; beds, trunks, bins; kneading-troughs for housewives, deed-boxes for scribes, merchants, rabbis. Such as a matter of fact are the various works which the Mishna reveals to us as carried on by carpenters." (*Science Sociale*, 1909, p. 30.)

prefer it, when I clap my hands, I know not what half-dressed actors will answer my summons altogether, to take their places in the impromptu play of which I am the dishevelled producer. Sooner than construct a scenario, I would rather introduce your own self into the midst of my company and leave you the bother of getting what you can out of it.

The first image that comes into my mind is that Archaic Greek Warrior's Head which I found in a New York auctioneer's catalogue. What is gripping about it is its intensely individual character, the terrifying sign of personality in the face, and at the same time its super-human aspect; a face at once concrete and geometrical, the meeting in a single line-theorem of the daintiest reciprocal propositions of Euclid and Pythagoras; a face both impassioned and hard-bitten. The relation for instance between the nose, which is the appraising-point of mastery in the middle of the face, and the two super-ciliary arcs chiselled like brackets in Algebra, is a thing of endless interest, almost of awe. You might say that the human material has been completely fined down and is wholly subordinated to the mind and the will. The face is the expression, the operation, the direct work of the mind, instead of being its cross-grained and venture-some translation.

The second picture is of quite a different character. A little vignette of the East on the edge of the desert; you see a group consisting of a man, a boy, an ass and a camel. The man is about to tether these animals to the trunk of a dried-up palm-tree, before going on his way with his son into the heart of the wilderness. Even now you anticipate my interpretation by suggesting how the ass of course signifies the imagination, and the camel the memory. For at the point we have got to, these two modest beasts of burden have outworn their usefulness. The ass a bag of trumpets whose monstrous organ is like the very voice of passion and despair, an ass living only on dried hay and hollow straw, with his vast ears and their million hairs as alive as those of Midas to every atmospheric change and every quiver of inspiration. The ass, fit mount for prophets, false ones as well as true, is the very imagination itself, a faculty with big velvet eyes. And as for the camel with his double sack on his back, and his complicated apparatus of cisterns and stomachs, what need have we henceforward of this four-footed alembic? And if I were in the place of the child himself, the dubious Isaac whom we have inwardly begotten to the likeness of our own contemplation, I should not feel entirely secure. What is the use in going to the desert and reaching the inner and inmost wilderness, as Exodus says, if it is merely to bring ourselves with us? What company more odious? Are we not sure to find in there at our service that goat entangled in the briars by the horns—a sacrifice from us to the Eternal?

Again the warrior's head from Magna Græcia has appeared upon the screen. But what takes my attention this time is the helmet on his head. Why do we always represent St. Joseph as a weather-beaten hall-porter whose soft-headed baldness cries out less for the halo than for the smoking-cap? And why should the halo itself always be in the shape of a luminous pancake? Why should not Christians come and call up in many ways the soldier of Christ and fit him out with the helmet proper to his calling? And why should I not draw you myself around my thought of St. Joseph that sort of steely sheath, that unyielding coif, surmounted by a triumphant volute partaking of that mathematic indestructibility of which his features just now took on the comport in our eyes? Then at once this consideration arises in our mind: St. Joseph was above all *the keeper of the Law.* It was in the shelter of the latter that the possibilities of the interior life unfolded in him.

"I am not come to destroy but to fulfil," says our Lord. Now which of us can boast of *fulfilling* perfectly the Commandments with the same faith and the same attention that he would show to the doctor's *orders* for instance? To lay down exactly for them the bounds which they have the right to exact, not just refraining from the contrary of what they require, but positively making them the motive, inwardly assimilated, of our outward behaviour. Thus it is that our Lord teaches us that the Commandment: "Thou shalt not commit adultery," forbids not only adultery and fornication, but every kind of bad thought. And what keeps out the bad thought if not the good? Who brings to our business as Christians that purity, that scrupulousness, that interest, that intensity and that simplicity in execution, that sort of clinging and pressing towards it of the heart and the mind effectively fulfilling and giving it meaning, form, efficacy, and virtue? Who can boast that he has raised obedience to the level of prescription and that he has properly coloured that dry plan of which the outline has been entrusted to us of those minute and detailed specifications of Exodus and Leviticus, the number of steps that can be made on the Sabbath, as later on the laws of the Church on fasting, on marriage, on the prohibition of butter during Lent, or of eating fish at the same time as meat (the Ember days always falling at the most awkward time)—all that made up a sort of artistic restriction on our liberty, a musical canvas, a tiny but delicate appeal to our attention and our force of character, an invitation to prefer the law of God to that of the flesh, a hair between Him and us as fine as the spirit, " One jot," says the Gospel, " one tittle " : Not only the jot which is the simplest of all letters, without any recoil upon itself, the finger pointing towards heaven, but the dot which is exactly superposed, that little star above the magnetised needle. And yet all those easy and wholesome Commandments which God has given us, not for His sake but for ours, those Commandments of which we are told that we are to fulfil them to overflowing—what a sorry mess we made of them before the Holy Father with heartbroken indulgence reduced them to the minimum so as to spare us the transgression ! With what ill-humour, what ill-grace, what slowness, what despairing eye on the way out, do we lend ourselves to those which have been left ! How differently we should behave if these prescriptions instead of being those of a most wise and kindly God, came from the masseur or the soothsayer ? Far from their facility being an aid to their fulfilment, it rendered them contemptible in our eyes. But Joseph who is *par excellence* he that keeps, he that watches, and preserves, he who in a good and faithful heart has received all the grain of the Sower without losing one particle, Joseph who is the *Just* man *par excellence*, keeps on repeating to himself the admonitions: " Swift as needles of fire " of the great Psalm 118:—

" Thy words have I hidden in my heart. . . . Blessed art thou, O Lord: teach me thy justifications. . . . I will meditate on thy commandments: and I will consider thy ways. . . . For thy testimonies are my meditation. . . . My soul hath coveted too long for thy justifications, at all times. . . . Give me understanding, and I will search thy law. . . . Thy judgments are delightful. Thy justifications were the subject of my song in the place of my pilgrimage. . . . It is good for me that thou has humbled me, that I may learn thy justifications. . . . Mine eyes have failed for thy words: When wilt thou comfort me? . . . All thy statutes are the truth. . . . How sweet are thy words to my palate! More than honey to my mouth! . . . Pierce thou my flesh [1] with thy fear. . . . I opened my mouth, and I panted, because I longed for thy commandments. . . . Thou art near, O Lord: and all thy ways are truth. . . . Seven times a day have I given praise to thee, for the judgments of thy justice. Much peace have they that love thy law: and to them is no stumbling-block. . . .

[1] The Latin says: " My fleshes "—*carnes meas*—every kind of flesh there is in me—all the ways I have of being fleshly.

I have kept thy commandments and thy testimonies: because all my ways are in thy sight."

Mandata Tua, and again *Mandata Tua*, *Lex Tua*, *Lex Tua*, *Lex Tua*, *Judicia Tua*.

So speaks the Patron of a happy death.

Washington, 1932.

THE THIRD MEETING

THE THIRD MEETING

(JOHN XXI, 1–14)

The third day after Easter Sunday, behold Peter suddenly cries: "I go a-fishing." With him there are Thomas who was called Didymus, and Nathanael of Cana who knows better to hold a sickle than an oar, and the sons of Zebedee, they of that country, and two other comrades. "They say to him: 'We also come with thee.' And they went forth and entered into the ship."

It is a long time since he chanced to go fishing. Three years they have been trailing together over all the roads of Judea and Samaria. And now it is over and what a finish! Or rather we cannot say it is over, it is the old life that little by little has shrunken and is gone from us in tatters, now there is nothing of it left, and something enormous and totally different has begun. It will not be a bad thing to go back to our country to get our ideas clear. It will be interesting to go over the doings of yore a little, just to see the difference. Besides we have been told to come here, nothing for it but to obey: "I go a-fishing!"

So Peter is back in his own country. It is as well that it is night just now. Yesterday what queer impressions! The house, the village, everything was there. We cannot say that anything is wanting, it is as well copied as in a painting. There is an old gate which has remained just the same as when I was quite small, I used to play at opening and shutting it I don't know how often. Even the people, we recognise them all, they have not changed much, curious how I begin to forget their names. Why do they put on this puzzled expression when we talk to them, after three minutes? At first you would think them quite pleased and then you have that embarrassed look, you cannot hold them after that. The house, the village, our parent's grave, how touching it all was! But as for living there again, nobody wants to: you don't live in a picture.

But fishing, oh yes, you can still do that. Why the taste is the same as ever. You might even say that it has only increased and multiplied. Time was when no better taker of fish than Simon Peter sailed the sea of Galilee. A fine night like this, not a breath stirring, almost warm, we can't stand that. It must be fairly rotten with fish in the spots I know. "I go a-fishing."

Not a bit of it, there are no fish. We found all the good spots of once upon a time. Not a fish. The water is deserted. And now it is beginning to dawn. You can start telling faces. That's Nathanael and that's John.

And look, there is a fire on the shore, someone is there. He has spoken, he is pointing. And all of a sudden John says: "It is the Lord." They already knew it.

Forthwith Peter who was naked, casts his garment about him and throws himself into the water so as to land sooner: "For they were not far from the land but as it were two hundred cubits—*quasi cubitis ducentis*"—Cubits suggesting the swimmer's reach.

The boat is the Church, with the Pope and the Apostolic College about him. It is not far from the land, from that shore where Christ is waiting, where we shall all land one day. Within His call. She is separated from Him by a perfect number: twice one hundred, the square of ten redoubled. In the Garden of Olives Jesus was separated from us by "a stone-throw," just far enough to be still within reach of our cast for us to be able to hurt Him, for something of ours to reach Him where we cannot go ourselves. As far as is a stone's throw, we have cast Him out. For what we throw with all our strength to make impression on Him, our stones, our prayers as well. Now He has again put between Himself and His Church the official distance, what is bound to remain the same, what He had determined when He was preaching of old at Capharnaum, the distance needed for faith and just a little delay needed for mercy. On each side of the spiritual barrier the exact measure of withdrawal, what keeps the one from seeing and the other from being seen, this plan for the whole stretch of Time, this empty frame which the centuries are coming to fill, the parallel beckoning by the law and the fulfilment, the Crescent of Revelation completing the Crescent of Belief to form the perfect circle, the two corresponding C's, the halves of O.

Peter brooks no delay, he throws himself into the water. But before so doing, he vests, like the Bishop before Mass as we see him donning from head to foot his pontifical vestments.

There is a fire upon the shore, a red point in the shadow, three burning coals, somewhat like the lamp of to-day burning before the Blessed Sacrament, or that seed of the New Fire which is blessed on Holy Saturday.

Peter has got there first. No more does he walk miraculously upon the water as erstwhile when the Master stretched out His hand. You may call it floundering, and his grey beard is streaming wet. It is a trifle awkward swimming in these garments which cling to you. The others follow by dint of oars, dragging a weight so heavy that it hinders their advent. Look out, lads !

For at the word of this unknown man in the shadow on the shore they have let down the net on the right. And when they try it, once the net is hauled to land, and it is a miracle that it is not broken, there are a hundred and fifty three great fishes. I say 153.

What are these hundred and fifty three great fishes ? and how does it concern us who read our Gospel in this April month of 1931, that there should have been one hundred and fifty three great fishes, or only one hundred and fifty two ? I ask you.

The early Fathers believe that everything in the Bible without exception was for our profit and our spiritual reflection. Like the Paschal Lamb eaten whole with intestines and meat and the calcined bones curiously pulverised. Or again it is like modern industry which extracts from no matter what any amount of saleable by-products, consequently all these remarkably precise figures are not without a reason, we must not let them go without an effort at least to get something out of them.

One five three being a number which does not stand by the operation of one prime factor, it may be a good idea to begin by cutting off the last figure, the three in the third column, which is offered to us outstanding as the arithmetical device which gives us all the rest: 15 is 3 times 5. Now we know that *three* is the root of all number, that abstract image of divinity on which all creation and particularly the soul of man, as St. Augustine shows, has been built up. This *three* added to the number two, is the whole figure of Adam translated into the geometric terms, the Cross, the Heart in the midst of the four limbs. *Two* cunningly inserted into the *three* and have we not the two eye-balls looking at you or the double opening of ears and nostrils? Do we not always find throughout nature this law of symmetry and response? *Three* is substance, framework, essential architecture; and *two*, is life, conscious, is the starting-point and plurification of all things, unity self engendering, the principle of selfness and otherness. All this makes *five*, the two hands this work-a-day reduction of ourselves to a fringe of fingers which we carry at the ends of our two arms.

To this nature of Adam there is added from without the blessing of God. The Trinity is blessing Its likeness and Its work, bestowing upon it something which carries both approval and commission. So the priest still to-day baptising and blessing does always in the name of the

Holy Trinity. Benediction is grace through the Word uniting Himself with nature, calling up in her the power and relish of something novel corresponding with the invitation addressed to her. Thus the overlapping benedictions of God in *Genesis* multiply vegetable and animal species and the whole race of man (*Genesis* xvi. 10). " Multiplying I will multiply thy seed " and in the *Psalms* (*Ps*. iv. 8) : By the fruit of their corn, of their wine and their oil are they multiplied. Corn, is substance, oil is the unction on the head of Jesus Christ, and wine is the spirit the Giver of Life. All this serves the hallowing of man, as is said in the Gospel of Pentecost : " I in the Father, you in Me, and I in you."

There are two blessings, natural and supernatural, one represented by the co-efficient, the other by the decimal (symbolised by the X or the circle O) ; one being reproduction, sum, and the other consummation ; one proportion and the other plenitude. This plenitude in praise is expressed by the CL Psalms, each ending in acclamation to the Trinity. And the plenitude of another kind is represented by the CL great fishes captured on the right hand in Peter's boat.

Fish, as we know, is the blason of Christ, His social badge so to speak, borrowed like that of modern firms and executives from the greek initials of His name and title. We see the Fish figuring everywhere in the paintings of the Catacombs, surmounted by a basket of loaves, in allusion to the five loaves and two fishes of the Gospels. The fish is *beneath* the bread as the *substance* beneath the species or appearances. And it is this same fish in the text of St. John that we see made ready on the shore by the hands of Our Lord at the time of the Apostles' landing. *Piscis assus, Christus passus* . . the priest at the altar at the moment of consecration. At Emmaus and in the Supper Room it was the Eucharistic Gift pure and simple. Here in this session of peculiarly ecclesiastical character, where Christ in the morning of time sits in the midst of His Apostles like the Bishop among his ordinands, it is a sort of object-lesson of the Sacrament, it is the first lecture in theology, a reasoned analysis of the miraculous event.

Christianus alter Christus. The Christian is an image of Christ, modelled to a given epoch and by a group of circumstances, and, inasmuch as from the old Adam he passes into the estate of Son of God, he realises in himself the initials of the everlasting Fish. Let him swim henceforward, free from earthly contact, in the pure waters of baptism and Grace, breathing the very element which upholds him. There the many-meshed net of the fisherman will seek them out and make them as erstwhile on the Mount of the Beatitudes the banquet of the gathered Peoples. Not like the small fry thrown back into their native pond, but the *great Fish* nourished into the likeness of Christ on His Flesh and His Blood, on His teaching and His love, worthy to feed the faithful unto the consummation of the ages, to share out His substance to them, to supply them with a certain image of Christ, eatable, fitting in with their general or particular needs, be they passing or constant. So St. Paul, whose Epistles are read to us at Mass, so the Martyrs and the Doctors,

St. Mary Magdalen, St. Augustine, St. Thomas, St. Bonaventure, St. Benedict, St. Francis of Sales and he of Assisi, St. Ignatius, St. Benedict Labre, St. Vincent de Paul, Bossuet, Ozanam, Newman, and Catherine Emmerich, the Curé of Ars, Don Bosco, St. Teresa of the Child Jesus. All this treasury of saints, all these stars, all this live coin from the inexhaustible sea of Galilee, the known and the unknown where we have but to let down our net, they are at our disposal and not 153, but a hundred and fifty three thousand, nay 153 millions! Hail to the big brothers! Hail to the big fish coming on amid a swarming little crowd like so many Suns trailing with them a whole retinue of stars! Hail the great rolling of the thunder from end to end of the firmament in the country of the *Psalms!*

. . . All these meetings which the Gospels of Easter week one after another recounts have the same twilight or auroral character. It always takes place between night and morning, between one season and another, and it is neither one nor the other. At that moment, when a break, a change of rhythm not altogether free from a secret syncopation arises in the sustained line of time. The bank is still covered with dead leaves, but here and there that vesture of the hermit earth streaked with bitter tufts of dandelion, with bunches of narcissus and jonquil, bundles of periwinkle, little innocent Easter lilies, green things and long greening boughs. There are no leaves on the trees as yet, but a kind of glowing smoke, the touches as it were of an airy pastel. You surmise that earth on every side is getting uneasy about her nuptial napery, that a great deal of white is to be unrolled and opened out, and that she is untying a pink ribbon as it were, with smile ineffable making ready for her first communion. It is Magdalen falling on her knees recognising Jesus in the semblance of the gardener. It is the holy women at the tomb being aware of the flitting of angels like the cathedral choir in the thick of a high Mass, all those angels piled on one another like those confused imaginings in the garden outlined behind the sharp lights of a broad shaft of sun. It is the Apostles solemnly communicating behind closed doors, on even terms with death. It is the mysterious refection on the shore of Genesareth. It is the two disciples in a sunken road encountering that obscure wayfarer and in that homely room the light that slowly grows in radiance about that hallowed mouth, thou hast recognised Him, fortunate son of Cleophas! And still the Gospel gives us to understand that before the recognition there is between the soul and its Jesus as it were a mute watchword a kind of austere counter-sign "Do not touch me!" Jesus makes as though to go further on, and we make believe not to recognise Him. All the same the tomb has come between. This apparition which melts the heart within me, how fleeting it is![1] Between Thee and me, my Jesus, the hour would be

[1] So delicate is the union that the *Canticle* compares it to the laying hold by a single hair, one of those at the back of the head. (*Cant.* 4, 9): The neck is what joins the head to the body and the limbs. In the head are placed the organs of song and speech.

right ill chosen for breaking this convention of silence ! [1]

" Jesus said to them : ' Come, and dine.' And none of them who were at meat durst ask him : Who art thou ? " so that the present state, so dainty and fine, of suspense and balance between one world and the other be not disquieted in either one sense or another. " Knowing that it was the Lord." (It is He : and yet the silence of the Apostles better than their voice fails not to question Him.) " And Jesus cometh and taketh the bread, and giveth to them, and the fish in like manner." And then there was no more need to question Him. " This is now the third time that Jesus was manifested to his disciples, after he was risen from the dead."

Washington, 1931.

[1] God proposes the mysteries of faith to our soul amidst cloud and darkness, so that we do not see the truth but only glimpse them, as oftentimes it happens that when the earth is covered with fog we cannot see the sun, but see only a little more brightness where the sun is. (St. Francis of Sales : *On the Love of God*, Book 2, Chap. 14.)

ON THE PRESENCE OF GOD

ON THE PRESENCE OF GOD

It is a commonplace of theology, ever since Saint Dionysius the Areopagite, that all we can know in this world about God, is *that He Is* and *what He Is not.* But we must be very careful not to exaggerate the meaning of this antithetical proposition, nor say that we know God merely by negations, leaving Him hanging in the void and cutting Him away from any relationship with the world He has made. Such a notion would not be far removed from heresy. We know God not only negatively, but positively, as Saint Bonaventure and all his school have strongly affirmed. When we learn from God *that He Is*, according to the revelation made to Moses from the Burning Bush, we attain the Essential in Him, the same Verb[1] which in us and in all created beings makes the groundwork of every sensible and intelligible particular. And when at the same time we say that we also know *what He Is not*, since there is a reason for each absence, we enrich our knowledge of God in that special measure by which He overfills or quite refuses the inadequate receiver. For not to be here or there is quite another thing from not being there at all. God is not this or that thing, but He Is *in* everything, or rather everything is *in* Him, as Saint Paul tells

[1] In French the Word is *le Verbe.* The French has been literally translated to bring out the play on the word.

us. When we summon all creatures one by one to proclaim their inability to exist by themselves, and their vocation to be present in such or such guise, to act for, to *represent* Absolute Being in the domain of the particular, and the Eternal in that of the transitory, we add our note, one voice more to the mighty gamut of our praise. Just as an actor is engaged to play what in fact *he is not*, though his interpretation be truthful. It is one more way for us of not being speechless amidst the Presence. One more way for Being to halt at Nothingness. One more end, one definition more.

When we know of God that *He Is* and *what He Is not*, we have revelation not only of a Verb, but of the Verb's tense. God is always Now, and it is in the Now that He is present to all things. It is in this Now of His that all things find their beginning and their end. He is Alpha and Omega, at once the compass and the circle. The Apocalypse develops the revelation of Exodus when it calls God Him Who *was* and *is* and *is to come* (in Greek this future is indicated by a past tense). He Who is what has always been, is the Father; He Who is what is, resemblance fixing identity, the Verb translating substance, is the Son; and He Who is to come, the thrill of love using up in one flash 'twixt the two Participants the whole possibility of being away from the immediate, is the Spirit.[1]

Finally, when we say of things that we use them for knowing *what He is not*, that it is their *raison d'être* to be *what He is not*, we understand that no single thing by

[1] A kind of intake-exhalation. Being, Speech, Life.

itself can exhaust the impossibility of all the rest. They must join hands around Him. They must constitute round about Him a body, a system (*sepes*), they must pass before Him lest He pass them by, all the words must weave into a phrase. The Light must shine in perfect darkness, and what serves not to receive it, must at least serve to give it back. Thus the Spouse of the *Canticle* (i. and iii.), questioning one by one the keepers of the City, asks if they be " He Whom her soul loveth,"[1] and with great joy hears them answer that they are not, and that if she would find Him, she must go out from them and into the place of His repose, to midmost noontide.

Thus far we have taken the knowledge of God somewhat on the abstract and objective side. Now we must turn back our gaze upon ourselves and study this knowledge in ourselves as an interior state.

Several schools of philosophy, Islamic, Hindu and even Christian, have denied, on grounds of the radical difference between God and His creature, that there could be from her towards Him knowledge properly so-called. But that view is condemned. Brute creatures themselves know God in a certain way, since they be apt to bespeak Him and to praise Him. How therefore should man lack more eminent knowledge? Just how wide and deep it is, the discourse of our Lord in St. John at the institution of the Eucharist has made plain to us: " I will that where I am, you also may be with Me. The Spirit of Truth . . . you shall know Him because He

[1] *Ne vagari incipiam post greges* (*Cant.* i. 6).

shall abide with you and shall be in you. You see Me, because I live, and you shall live. In that day you shall know that I am in the Father and you in Me and I in you. If anyone love Me. . . . We will come to him and will make Our abode with him. The Paraclete . . . will teach you all things, and will bring all things to your mind, whatsoever I shall have said to you. . . . Thou knowest all things and needest not that any man should ask Thee: By this we believe that Thou camest forth from God. This is Life Eternal, that they know Thee the only true God and Jesus Christ (thus Life Eternal is likened to a knowing). That they all may be one, as Thou, Father, in Me, and I in Thee, that they all may be one in Us. The glory which Thou hast given to Me, I have given to them. I in them and Thou in Me, that they may be made perfect into One. I will that where I am, they also . . . may be with Me; that they may see My glory which Thou hast given Me. . . . That the love wherewith Thou hast loved Me, may be in them, and I in them."

Upon such texts as these theology has based the sublime theory of the transfiguring or deific Vision. So there is no doubt that after death we shall see God, as the Apostle says: not "in part," nor "as in a glass," nor "as in guesswork," nor by "conclusion, inference," but "face to face." Even in this life and amidst the veils which wrap us round, there is in us an aptitude for God, a seedling sustenance of our knowledge to be, the reminder of that substantial gaze upon Him to Whom we owe our being, that name in us, that personal calling-up which serves as gathering-ground for the scattered elements of our body. This spark[1] which slumbers in us, or rather which wakes while we slumber. There is in the depth of us a King's Son who has never lost memory of that drop of famous wine or of that clove of garlic which erstwhile his mother rubbed upon his lips, of that salt of ardour set upon our tongue the day of our baptism. There is in us a something mysteriously made fast, an *abode* meet to bear the indwelling of God (for how could He make a home of what passes away?), a persistence in existing, a kind of metaphysical regard upon the present from which our person draws the nourishment of its continuity.

Let us borrow a grisly parable from a half-mad book, just as in a sharp ascent one does not look too closely at the quality of the vantage which allows one to gain with a twist of the hip the three or four inches indispensable. In his *Chants de Maldoror*, the luckless Lautréamont supposes God Almighty to have visited a prostitute's den and there lost a hair of His head. The madman glues his eye to the graceless door and describes the writhing and despair of the forgotten strand trying to get back to its owner. Such is the soul of man, stagnated, blinded, and imprisoned under the crushing weight of original sin. She is not God, she is not a particle of God, since God has no parts, yet God is *in* her and in a certain way she cannot help being in Him

[1] *Tertiam proprietatem scintillam animae appellat quae est animae naturalis quaedam introrsus in suam originem propensio.* (Ruysbroeck in *Spec.*, *Div. Ver.*)

as her abiding cause: She belongs to Him, she is *indebted* to Him for existence, she is keeping back from Him an image which she must restore, there is unceasingly born in her an image which constitutes her existence, she calls to It and It calls to her, she dimly maintains with it an intimate live relationship; in the depth of a nameless separation, of dreadful darkness, she keeps miserably juxtaposing her twin birth with her Eternity.

When by unimaginable good fortune the soul so lost and crucified gets at last to hear something of that essential name which the Divine Lover imperceived keeps both suggesting to her and claiming her by, shall it be told her that she is not really capable of knowing anything of Him Who has touched her so nearly? She knows what she needs to know. Like the heroine in the Legend she replies to curious *how* and importuning *why: Just because it was I and because it was He*. Like Magdalen falling to her knees she forthwith answers the call with an attitude. What she did in ignorance, she now does with attentiveness. She tries by a series of little patient efforts to get into an attitude in which she may be able to hear better and better. She tries to understand and to apply with patience the advice given her and the vital necessity of listening. She tries to help God and to set herself with regard to Him, in a state of co-naissance. It is not this or that organ of sense or of understanding that she has to practise, it is herself in answer to smooth touches, that has to key her essence to a given disposition. And it is this disposition, behaviour, control in relation to God, not of our sense or our intelligence, but of the stream, the course[1] of being in us, which provides for the functioning of both intelligence and sense, this is what we call *knowledge*.

In this double work where our intelligence and will on the one hand, and Grace Divine on the other, act in loving harmony, our part is most especially to reduce the obstacles, and that of Grace is to exhale invisibly in the depth of us counsel and strength, to husband with occult benevolence our funds till the moment comes for her to play directly on us and add to the dim prompting of the voice the luminous summons of the face at last, according to the invitation of the *Canticle :* " Show me thy face, and let thy voice sound in mine ear." That voice so long mute ! That song so cruelly withheld ! For at that moment, according to the word of Isaiah, " our justice " shall go before our face.[2]

This ablative or reductive action shall be my theme in the first place. Isaiah, on the Saturday after Ash-Wednesday,[3] gives us the triple formula when he says : " If thou wilt take away the chain out of the midst of thee—and cease to stretch out the finger—and speak that which profiteth not." Let us examine this triple clause.

Taking away the chain from the midst : we need but recall what we know of motor-car and bicycle, and at once we understand what is called *throwing off gear*. Let us look closer at the Prophet's meaning. When we begin

1 *Viderunt te aquae, Deus, viderunt te aquae* (*Ps.* lxxvi. 17).
2 *Is.* lviii. 8.
3 *Is.* lviii. 9.

to enter on interior ways, the mental mechanism (the wheel within the wheel), from which we have withdrawn our outward usage, goes on functioning by itself. Ideas, fancies, recollections, motions of the intelligence, the feeling, the will, persist in holding strongly together like an unbreakable chain. All this goes in us like clockwork, or, if you prefer, a belt of buckets filling and emptying in the same tank. But when we have taken on the habit of God a little more, the depth of our mind remaining still and recollected, then the disjointed and half-dispelled distractions merely float idly like a cloud, tiresome for that matter, on the surface of the mind. There is no longer any bond between them, no more the chain, no more that self-acting drag that reunites them. In other words, the Will and the Imagination are no longer bound together by the bond of habit. There is a gap, a fissure, through which the Divine Lover has " put in His hand " (*Cant.* v. 4) (that Hand was the first of Jesus Christ that Saint Teresa saw objectively). That iron collar riveted to our neck, and chained to our middle, which kept us doubled up like the paralytic in the Gospel, is broken. We have other interests than contemplating the navel. " Ananias took the chain . . . from the neck of Jeremiah " (*Jer.* xxviii. 10). (Ananias, by the way, is the name of that good man of Damascus who delivered Paul from his blindness.)

Now let us go on to the second point: " If thou cease to stretch out the finger," says Isaiah. This outstretched finger is what we call the index. It is the sign used by printers to call attention to this or that paragraph.

The finger is both a line and a point. It serves to guide our attention. It fixes it on this or that object picked out by the eye, it unifies us, solidifies our joints in this or that direction. There is in us, as it were, an officer who shows his troops such and such a point as the aim of their endeavour, and it is this point beyond ourselves that compels the interior disposition we have to make. This outstretched forefinger is index of the tension of all our being towards a particular object chosen out of many. So Grace in us must see about holding back that archer ever ready to let slip his bolt. "Let not him that bendeth, bend his bow" (*Jer.* li. 3). Or, if there is anything to bend, let it be that mighty bow and peaceful which upholds cathedrals. "His bow rested upon the strong" (*Gen.* xlix. 24).

So the first counsel of Isaiah is to dismantle; the second to hold back; now let us look at the third, which is "to cease from speaking that which profiteth not."

It concerns interior words, that ceaseless ferment within us of images, words, thoughts, memories, desires, motives, germs and leavings. Our mind is like a fan, winnowing all that over and over. Or rather let me take the simile of a liquid on the fire. Over the enkindled flame of our mind all those things boil and boil in great bubblings, throwing off blinding vapours. The *Book of Exodus* tells us that "the river brought forth a boiling abundance of frogs" (*Exod.* viii. 3). The river is, as they say, the current life. The frogs are empty words lying low in its back-waters and its swampy margins, in that mud made by the mind mixing with concrete reality, and without respite making din after the word of *Proverbs :* " The face of the foolish boils over with folly." This clamour is not only insistent, it is noxious ; not only frogs does our inmost drain bring forth, but birds of the air in the Parable, devouring the seed of the Sower, rats setting off to dig it up. " And in the villages and fields in the midst of that country there came forth teeming hordes of mice " (*I Kings* v. 6). It is this unrest in us that we must soothe or gradually render inoffensive. It is this ill-ease, this constant striving with our bars, this flight, this impatience of the touch of God that we must master, regulate, reduce. The Sabbath rest must reign from end to end of our inward cantonments, a consecrated rest, a delicate exquisite suspense. " If thou turn away thy foot from the Sabbath," says Isaiah, that is, the longing to be elsewhere, " from doing thine own will in My holy day " (*Is.* lviii. 13).[1]

Lo ! as I finish penning these words, I plunge my hand into my pocket and draw out my beads ! Is not that the very image of this chain which we are enjoined to " take away from the midst of us ? "[2] All those holy

[1] This is pointed out by the Fourth Commandment, which stipulates : " On the Sabbath Day, thou shalt do no works, neither thou nor the stranger within thy gates." This *stranger* is the external disquietudes which we keep in the depths of our memory.

[2] The Rosary may be suggested by the fifty golden rings which used to catch up the curtains of the Tabernacle, " that might catch the loops of the curtains and might make one tabernacle " (*Exod.* xxxvi. 13). As to the two little chains of fine gold to hold the Rational on the breast of the High Priest, it seems as though we must see there an image of the two Testaments with their intertwining texts. Perhaps it is the Rosary in the hand of the Angel of the Apocalypse that binds the Dragon for a thousand years.

words interlocking, are they not the counterpart of that baleful concatenation of inane syllables?

And how shall we do about "stretching out the finger," the finger *par excellence* which is the index, when we use it with the thumb to reckon our interior treasure, to pass through the pinch of our apprehension all the jewels of that crown of praise? What surer way of laying silence on the frogs than to put rhythm instead of chaos, the word which profiteth for that "Which profiteth not," thus betraying its diabolic kinship? When we get our thoughts into step, into regular cadence, we thrust from off our beat the unseasonable elements. "By degrees the wind grows quiet," and the celestial dove, seeing us bent on business, takes heart and comes nigh to those auricular approaches which we wear, not in the middle of the face, but on each side of the head.

We have examined the purgative part of prayer wherein our will has the more evident share; I mean the reduction of obstacles. We now have to turn our endeavour after expression to the positive side, remembering that after all it is the privilege of poets and fools to set foot boldly down where wise men fear to hazard the tip of their toe. Here it is not a matter of a saint charitably trying, by reversing his steps in his own footprints, to make practicable the approach to his own property, but of an adventurer who upon hints from Scripture and with no mirth-moving pretensions[1] is

[1] I am sure to be asked: Why speak of things which you admit to be beyond your experience and comprehension? I make three answers: (1) Nothing here is of my own. I only

embarking on an expedition of inference and reconnaissance.

The different zones or atmospheres, successive, dare I say? which surround the settled residence of God in our heart's depth, may be designated by the names Peace, Light, Nourishment, Principle, Justice.

Peace such as God gives is not merely a negative quality, an absence of pain, of difficulty, struggle, regret and longing, although by the radical disappearance of all that we acquire a new feeling of ease, of enlargement and of liberty. But I mean that the peace of God in us

compendiate and bring together the showings of the Bible, the Fathers and the Mystics whose evidence hangs together so remarkably; (2) Christianity is not an esoteric doctrine, there is no part of it set apart for the few. All belongs to everyone. Thus we see the saints trying to put themselves within reach of the lowliest, to make practicable to them the way and the advance which has been successful to themselves. What blame can there be for trying to aid them in this enterprise? (3) The great need of modern man is prayer, interior life, recovering at any cost relationship with God. We are all dying of hunger and thirst. Now in the interior life there are no watertight bulkheads. All hangs together. The most mediocre Christian shares the atmosphere breathed by Saint Bernard and Saint John of the Cross.

The dogma of the Communion of Saints puts him at one with their virtues and their contemplation. It is not a question here of human science, but of a more or less complete assent to a love and a light. Though we may not be able to follow Saint Teresa, a secret thrill warns us that we are in communication with her, that she is stirring a little further on in a territory which is ours. We have the right and the duty to profit by the Saints, to not leave them alone, to make use of their explorations and their discoveries, to follow them in intelligence and desire if we cannot otherwise. To penetrate into the interior life we cannot rest the eye on our own feet. It is the star we must not lose sight of. It is the whole horizon, with the successive planes which it bounds ,that we must get into our head.

infuses something new and positive. We have seen how it is the image of the Sabbath, of that Seventh Day when God, having created the world and found all the works of His hand *valde bona*, enters on a rest populous evermore with eyes. Thither are we invited to follow Him, saying after the fashion of the Blessed Virgin: "In all things have I sought rest, and in the inheritance of the Lord will I linger" (*Eccles.* xxiv. 11), and a little further on: "I am become in His presence as one that findeth peace" (*Cant.* viii. 10). But what peace? "My peace" saith the Lord (*John* xiv. 27), "Not as the world giveth." "The peace," Saint Paul goes on, "which passeth all understanding." That which goes before God's presence, when, all doors being shut, He takes session in our soul, saying: "Peace be to you. It is I" (*Luke* xxiv. 36), and that which flows from His words when He says: "These things have I told you that in Me you may have peace" (*John* xvi. 33). The repose of the Christian soul is an approbation and an acquiescence. She approves of all things, and of herself, in Whom they are "very good," that is, inasmuch as they are the work of God. Peace, therefore, is founded on a rooted humility, on a profound abstention, not from co-operation, but from concurrence. The soul, with a shudder of joy, takes cognisance of that blissful nothingness which forbids her to see any more in herself and all things else aught but the work of her Creator. That is her point of view henceforward. Thither have so many pathways led, nothing remains to her but according to the counsel of the Prophet to draw back from them her feet. Let the friends who seek her be amazed, therefore, if they will, like the fox in the fable, at all those footprints going in the same direction and not one that turns back. Have we not taken care, following the self-same counsel of Isaiah, to close behind us the approach to all those dangerous tracks? Behind that invisible and impassable barrier, such as for instance the religious vows, interposing henceforth between us and the world, we can, like workmen mending a road, go on tranquilly with our labour. We utilise for rest what seemed made only for traffic. "And thou shalt be called repairer of the fences, turning the pathways into rest" (*Is.* lviii. 12).

The second aureola which decks the presence of God in the depth of our heart, figured by those crowns and shroudings of pure gold about the Mercy-Seat, is very properly called *light*. "God said: Let there be Light! And there was Light" (*Gen.* i. 3). In His dealings with our interior world, the first thing to do for God is to see clear these. God, to call the soul to life, uses the self-same word as He used to create the world: "Let there be Light!" "There was," says Saint John, "a true light which enlighteneth every man that cometh into this world. In Him was life, and the life is the light of men." Note how Saint John does not use the present but the imperfect: "There was a light." The light I used to call men into life, is still there, it is not quenched, there is but to set about seeking it, there is still a way to make use of it. There is a way to bring it out again after momentary occultation. "In His hands," says the Book of Job, "He hideth the light, and commandeth it to come again." (Hands meaning the operation and assiduities of Grace), "He sheweth His friend concerning it, that it is His possession, and that he may come up to it" (*Job* xxxvi. 32, 33). But what then is this light which answers the call of light? Not brought in from without, it is in the depth of us it springs. The soul uses for her answer the self-same word addressed to her, she is own sister to that very question put to her. She passionately declares to God that He alone exists, and that she is there only to make believe veraciously that she is other than He. She confesses the uncreated Light by virtue of this light which He has made. "With Thee is the fount of Life," says the thirty-fifth *Psalm*. "Then shall thy light break forth as the morning . . . and thy darkness be as the noonday," says Isaiah (lviii.). By the urgency of her Beloved, suddenly the soul has snatched herself from darkness. "God saw the light that it was good, and He divided the light from the darkness," and He called the light Day and the darkness Night (*Gen.* i. 4, 5). Of that darkness which is her own element she fashions the instrument of her confession. It is darkness that affords her nourishment, form, and voice. "Night," says the *Psalm* cxxxviii. 11, "shall be my light in my pleasures."

God has ranged the darkness round about us to keep us from seeing anything but this light. "God made darkness His covert" (*Ps.* xvii. 12). Of our opacity He has made a mirror. He has set it within as in a vessel. It is that night which constitutes the *dark room*, which permits the distinct formation of ideas. Darkness it is which allows us to form into words and prayers that fertilising breath which God blends with our original nothingness. "What I say to you in the dark, tell it in the light" (*Matt.* x. 27). And we will sum up all this paragraph by saying that in this abode, where God goes on in us by means of His countenance [1] to a second creation, He brings to our darkness a gift of re-birth within us as inexhaustible as His eternity. *O oriens!*

As God has given us life, "the true light which enlighteneth every man that cometh into the world" (*John* i. 9), "Causing fire to break out in the midst of him" (*Ezek.* xxviii. 18) (*fire* meaning that devouring light of conscience which is the delight of the elect and also the punishment of the reprobate), so also it is He Who preserves it in us.[2] As He is light, He is equally

[1] "If then the light that is in thee be darkness" (*Matt.* vi. 23).
"A light shined in the room" (*Acts* xii. 7).
"He will bring forth thy justice as the light" (*Ps.* xxxvi. 6).
"Who called you out of darkness into His marvellous light" (*I. Pet.* ii. 9).
"The light of Thy countenance is signed upon us" (*Ps.* iv. 7).
"To the righteous a light is risen up in darkness" (*Ps.* cxi. 4).
"He bringeth up to light the shadow of death" (*Job* xii. 22).
"I form the light and create darkness" (*Is.* xlv. 7).

[2] I call to mind a text of the Psalms bearing on this: *Sicut crassitudo terrae erupta est super terram, dissipate sunt ossa nostra secus infernum.* (*Ps.* cxl. 7). The crust is that rigid mineral shell of bad habit in which sin petrifies us, turning into a grotesque idol the child of God. It is that hard mask which the working of Grace in us shatters, warming, dilating our liquid interior unto the dislocation of our bones, unto the re-building of our whole architecture. Is it not said of God that "His jealousy is hard as hell?" (*Cant.* viii. 6).

nourishment. " Come to Me," saith the Lord, " and I will refresh you " (*Matt.* xi. 28), in answer to that prayer of the faithful soul begging God to " refresh her bowels " (*Philemon* 20). " For My flesh is meat indeed, My blood is drink indeed " (*John* iv. 34). But it will not be meat *indeed* for you without your collaboration, as Samson's riddle gives us to understand: " Out of the eater came forth meat " (*Judges* vi. 57). And our Lord a little further on counsels us to " provide " ourselves, to " labour for the food " (*John* vi. 27). What food? Not " that which perisheth," but the supersubstantial bread, the "bread surpassing bread" (*Eccles.* xxxvi. 20), "which endureth unto life everlasting, which the Son of Man will give you." It is the food He Himself uses when He says: " I have meat to eat which you know not " (*John* iv. 32), " to do the will of Him that sent Me " (*ibid.* 34).

On the other hand, there are texts to quote in plenty referring to the presence of Christ under the species of drink; but we will keep this wine, as at the marriage-feast of Cana, for another moment, " until we drink it new " (*Matt.* xxvi. 29). Let us get back to that substantial feast which we see laid for us on every page of Scripture, that spiritual merry-making to which the Good Shepherd herds His sheep scattered the world over. For it is the bread that makes the Church.

The fog, the smoke, that cold and heavy vapour arising from the ground when the wind is not breathing, that shifty element having the twofold effect of blanketing and bewraying vision; that criss-cross enmeshing our feet, dimming our pathway, dividing from our brethren, which keeps us from seeing beyond our nose what our hands cannot grip or our stick prod, behold the cloud in whose midst Ezekiel (xxxiv. 12) shows us all mankind scattered and lost, with the Lord in search of His sheep. But just where sight no longer serves, the internal mechanism of craving and digesting, the apprehensive scent, the suction of vital breath which the Creator has set in their nostrils serve to guide these poor animals. In spite of deceptive appearances, the stupidest wether, the heaviest-horned ram, refuse to eat sand. Since they fail to know where they are, the Angels send the spring to meet them. From Alps unseen, right to their heart exhales a verdant breath, all manner of violets and cuckoo-buds, the pure cool narcissus, the rude flavour of the dandelion, all seethed in virtues of the wet earth, numberless little honey-bells so sweet that the flies are at a loss what to do with them, a velvet of young days, a tender thing like cream. Then out of the desert *tundra*[1] come running unnumbered herds of beasts, and God breaks His rest to listen to that browsing, that clacking of tongues and lips, that mighty noise of crunching jaws. He looks on France and from every village He gets the breath of that soup a-steaming up. He marvels at all our ways of tasting and at all the tastes we get. But when the body is profiting by so many dishes, shall the spirit only, despite that prayer which Our Father Himself has taken care to teach us, be baulked

[1] "Cursed be the man that trusteth in man: he shall dwell in dryness, in the desert, in a salt land and not inhabited" (*Jer.* xvii. 5–6).

of its refreshment? Is there not behind the mist beyond the torrent a Holy Land whose innocent breathings come to us in gusts with a muffled sound of bells? Nay, it is that very torrent, none the less irresistible for all its noiselessness, that itself takes up the exploration on our behalf. How fail to notice that we are already afloat, we have but to yield to the drift, to that unbroken rapid! Notwithstanding rocks and shoals, the current is the stronger, and will wash us more or less soaked and shaken over all the bars, even beyond those treacherous dykes all choked with weed, whence you think we shall never get free. And now behold the river broadening and a land right spacious, past the thirteen States between the Alleghanies and the Rockies fringing the Mississippi, given us to eat. The table is laid, we have but to partake. God is giving Himself to us, farther than the eye can reach, plain and mountain, bluff and valley, grazing-ground and wilderness, in triumphal vista without end! It is for the entering in. Lo! then, that Land which Joshua told us of, "flowing with milk and honey" (*Jos.* v. 6). No fear that we shall ever have done exploring it. "Thy mandate is exceeding vast," says *Psalm* cxviii. "We are come into a spacious land," says the *Book of Judges* (xviii. 10), "watered," says *Isaiah*, "by rivers without bounds." "Who hath measured?" says *Ecclesiasticus* (I. 2) and *Job* (xi. 9) says that "His measure is longer than the earth and wider than the sea." "God heard me unto enlargement," says *Psalm* cxvii. Such enlargement and to such a scale that "the span of Cherub-wings" (*Is.* viii. 8) alone can give the proportion. "Who shall tell us the breadth of God?" again says St. Paul. "There shall Israel pasture," says *Hosea* (iv. 16), "a wide land where the tillers shall go astray."[1] Inhabit the earth and thou shalt feed upon the richness thereof (*Ps.* xxxvi. 3, 4).

"I will be satisfied," says *Psalm* xvi., "when Thy glory shall appear." That flood of comestible knowledge, which the horizon up about us like a mighty plate, which the earth's massy hump as it turns, keeps crumbling into our maw even to the roots of our tongue, that succulent herbage, that ocean of standing-corn, that tablecloth whereon are heaped for us the "blessings" of the sky, of the waters, and of "the deep that is under" (*Gen.* xlix. 25), the roast, the iced, relieved with most exquisite seasoning, all is nothing to us compared with that drop of godly sap at Abraham's finger-tip, for which we are a-thirst, compared with that scrap of manna. It is not bread we want, but the essence of bread, that mysterious *fatness* of the grain[2] spoken of by *Psalm* cxlvii., that food to whose relish Saint Paul invites us by a certain "appetite for the things above" (*Col.* iii. 2).[3] that "spare bread" (*Is.* xxx. 20), as though unseen "beneath the ashes" (*III Kings* xix, 6, and *Exod.* xii. 30), that coin of eternity, that luminous clandestine rondure which the priest at every daybreak slips between our lips. Well for the man to whom Christ has tendered

[1] "Thou hast set my feet in a spacious place" (*Ps.* xxx. 9).

[2] "All the fat shall be the Lord's by a perpetual law" (*Lev.* iii. 16).

[3] "He that eateth, eateth to the Lord" (*Rom.* xiv. 6).

those species alive with His own Substance ! " For not by bread alone doth man live, but by every word proceeding from the mouth of God " (*Matt.* iv. 4). Bread and word of life, giving life evermore to him that receiveth (*John* vi. 59). The teeth, like the intelligence, may do their work of division upon this divine helping, the tongue pressing it against the palate may get its inner savour, our own moisture may mingle with it, but only on the altar of the heart in the tabernacle of the bosom between the breasts will it enkindle a fire of power and a light of contentment. " My words will not pass away," the Son of God tells us, as if in writing. Let us then, like the poor woman troubled with issue of blood, afflicted with that perpetual flow which never lets us " continue in the same state " (*Job* xiv. 2), cling " to the hem of His garment " (*Matt.* ix. 20), and listen, in that pause of time which the specialists call *ecstasy*, to that word of sovereign establishment, that affirmation of the eternal Presence : " Fear not, have confidence, it is I, I am He."

Up to now I have only described, or rather so far as I could have indicated, the fruits of God's presence in us. It now remains for us according to the invitation addressed to Zacheus perched above on the tree of Genesis, to " come down " (*Luke* xix. 5), and consider this house wherein it has pleased the Saviour to establish *to-day* and this very instant His abode. The moment is come to penetrate the domain of causes and roots, and go right to our foundations by the way of humility. And at once this dazzling and heroic idea breaks upon us with the violence of absurdity: He is not come to us, it is we who come to Him! "Before we were, He was!" We partake in Him of His own way of beginning. As the Buddhists [1] have well seen, we may go down to the bottom of self by all the rungs of introspection without meeting anything but fluid element, volatile and inconsistent, movement from potency to act, until we lay hands on being's self, on that acting image of God in us which is substance, cause, spirit, and life which the sacred books call essentially *firmamentum* (*Ps.* xviii. 2). "God," says the *Book of Kings*, "has become" my firmament. A principle translated to an activity. *Opera manuum ejus annuntiat firmamentum* (*Ps.* xviii. 2). It is the principle which the Lord promulgated in the beginning of the days (*Gen.* i. 6): "Let there be a firmament made amidst the waters, and let it divide the waters from the waters." That is: Let the principle in every creature, which is both solidity and separation, command the mobile elements until that particular figure of His perfection be realised which the Lord desires to obtain from us,[2] and in which they find equilibrium and stability.[3] We must go down to the bottom of ourselves before we find the stainless blue.[4] And since we are one with Jesus Christ as the numbers are with the Head, it

[1] *Ps.* cxxxvi. 7: *Exinanite, exinanite usque ad fundamatum in eo.*

[2] Naturally, this verse of mystery bears other meanings.

[3] "Thou hast founded the earth upon its own bases" (*Ps.* ciii. 5). "My substance is as nothing before Thee" (*Ps.* xxxviii. 6). "My substance is with Thee" (*ibid.* xxxviii. 8). "He hangeth the earth upon nothing" (*Job* xxvi. 7).

[4] "Behold, I will lay thy foundations in sapphires" (*Is.* liv. 2).

is from the Word Himself that we are authorised to borrow the words of the final Pasch: "Holy Father, I will that where I am, they also may be with Me. That they all may be one, as Thou, Father, in Me, and I in Thee; that they also may be one in Us. Glorify Me with the glory which I had, before the world was, with Thee." "Then," says the sanctified soul, "I shall know as I am known," says that pure image in the depth of us, that Conception in which it has been made capable of calling upon the Father.

This glory which we give to the Creator, the personal tribute which we are capable of bringing to Him, is transparency. The vision of God is in us accompanied by the discernment of that in us which is not Him, that is, of our own nothingness: "In Thy truth," says *Psalm* cxviii. 75, "Thou hast humbled me." Beyond the contingent, the strange and the accidental, we have found again our nature essential and profound, the resonance beseeming that pass-word which, handed on from generation to generation, has set us up. "He shall raise up," says Isaiah (lviii. 12), "the foundations of generation and generation." At the touch of the reality in which we were born [1] the idol in whose image we re-made ourselves, melts away; the falsehood in us feels the crumbling of the complicity covenanted between our passions and our perverted understanding. The building piled up, overloaded, goes to wrack and ruin. It is the spirit lusting victoriously against the flesh, it is

[1] "Whatsoever is first-born of all flesh shall belong to thee" (*Numbers* xviii. 15).

venturous matter starting to boil with the heat of the Commandment, it is primal nature dilating and cracking the shell of second nature.[1] "The fountains have appeared," says *Psalm* xvii. 16, "and the foundations are uncovered." It is the heart in sudden eruption. It is the seal of the "sealed fountain" breaking away! It is the sinful woman, Magdalen or Eve Lavallière, suddenly seeing herself and watering with torrential tears those Saving Feet upon her. How she understands now that word which the Prophet himself addresses to her: "I will water thee with my tears, O Hesebon!" (*Is*. xvi. 9). With passion she embraces that lowliness, that radical self-detestation, "that altar of earth" on which God has taught us in *Exodus* (xx. 24) that He wills to be honoured, that earth of which she is made, that handful of ashes which is all that belongs to her and all that she can give. Weeping, she tenders to the Master that medal of sin which she has at last decided to tear from off her neck.

Is it possible to go further still? Will not this residence at the bottom of our heart entail consequences somehow legal, and when God takes over all our being to "re-invest" it after His fashion that is not from without but from within, will He not bring all His rights with Him, and the fullness of His inheritance as Son co-equal with the Father? Will not the deed entail the title? Will not the usage imply the right? Will not the inspiration demand the utterance? Shall the Word cease to be "with God" because of being at the same

[1] "Then shall thy light break forth as the morning" (*Is*. lviii. 8).

time with us? "That which I see with My Father," says *John* (viii. 38), "I speak." Yours to do.[1] Yours to achieve in time what in the depths of you I witness in those words which cannot pass away (*Matt.* xxiv. 35). "The Holy Spirit will teach you all things, and bring all things to your mind, whatsoever I shall have said to you" (*John* xiv. 26). Between Time and Cause, will not the Heart of Jesus become for us Interpreter of Eternity and the Instrument of our Resurrection ever new in the present? Between Time and Eternity is He not the source of our continuity and the mainstay for our resistance? He is the shore and the rock to which the faithful people cling when they have crossed the sea of material elements and the flood of Time, *fluenta Jordanis* [2] which guards the Promised Land. He is that "New Man" of whom Saint Paul speaks, whom we shall have to put on after the plunge of the second Baptism. And in the end all this gear of sense which serves our outward life here below and wraps us like a tunic, can no longer serve us just as it is where we are going. We must change our dress. We must put on another adapted to our new relations, the "nuptial garment" of the Parable. "I have put off my garment, how shall I put it on?" says the Spouse of the *Canticle*. Not that we lose anything, but we are complete. I do not want to be unclothed, but to be clothed upon, says

[1] Yours, your turn to accomplish those works which speak for you. "I tell my deeds to the King" (*Ps.* xliv. 2). "Thou hast wrought all our works in us" (*Is.* xxvi. 12).

[2] "Pass thy land as a river, O daughter of the sea" (*Is.* xxiii. 10).

Saint Paul. Behold established " the new man, that mortal which has put on immortality " (*I Cor.* xv. 54).

This is indicated in the parable of Isaac and his two sons, a meaning which it bears among several others (*Gen.* xxvii.). Jacob the supplanter clutching the heel of his twin-brother, is the Divine Free-booter, our secret partner, later-born in fact, anterior by right. He it is, Who when the Father says: " My Son ! " takes upon Himself to answer in us: *Adsum.* He it is, Who in order to deceive that Father now unable to see and knowing only by touch,[1] and so as to get back that birthright which Red Satan in the beginning of the Ways let go, covers His Flesh with the sheathing of a slaughtered kid.[2]

" The hands, the hands," said the Patriarch twice over, " are the hands of Esau, but the voice, the voice is the voice of Jacob." That voice in which he discerns an echo of the voice of Abel. That voice which is the

[1] Inaccessible to our sight, but not to our contact.

[2] " Lo ! Adam is become as one of us " (*Gen.* iii. 22). It is the case of Adam and Eve expelled from Paradise, whom God Himself mysteriously clothes in a coat of skin. Where did those garments come from if not from dead animals? How so, dead, since the dread Visitant had not yet found his way into Paradise? Here begins the mystery. Adam, having learned that Christ was his substitute in the atonement for sin, made for himself instead, perhaps by God's orders, a figurative outline of the sacrifice to come, a lamb, says Origen, whom he immolates to God, of which the fleece served to cover his limbs, so figuring Christ, our victim, our ransom, Who having taken on " the likeness of sinful flesh," offered Himself to clothe us Himself with His merits and His justice. Thus has the Redeemer been shown forth by " the Lamb slain from the beginning of the world " (St. Augustine, *Enchiridion*).

organ of the Word. "Let thy voice sound in mine ears," says the Spouse of the *Canticle*, "for it is sweet to me!" The voice of that conception in us, which the power of the Most High hath overshadowed (*Luke* i. 35). For, "in the shadow of him whom my soul desired, I sate me down" (*Cant.* ii. 3).

So take courage, usurping soul, from the thought that thou art dealing with a God Whose goodness keeps Him from seeing clear. The whole Bible is full of nothing but blind Patriarchs, and no doubt it was the news of the paternal dimness that gave legs to the Prodigal Son. Too well we know that when we throw ourselves into His arms, His eyes will serve Him but for weeping. If those dropped eyelids dim Him not enough, Veronica has brought her veil, and the soldiers of the prætorium their blindfold, without which the sceptre, the crown and the purple mantle might only intimidate us. Not by the eyesight does the Father recognise His work, but by the touch.[1] "*Intuetur cor*" (*I. Kings* xvi. 7). Only from the heart does He ask the secret of our sonship. He inhales to find what odour we have. And if it be not that of good works, of that "fertile field" (*Gen.* xxvii.), whose fruit He expects of us, at least it will be the irresistible fume of that incense in which our Christian profession has enfolded us. "The smell of thy garments," says the *Canticle* (iv. 11),

[1] "As many as touched Him were made whole" (*Mark* vi. 56). "Approach Esther, and touch the sceptre" (*Esther* xv. 14). "Everyone that shall touch it shall be made holy" (*Exod.* xxix. 37).

is "as frankincense." Then shall we know with Him so great darkness, that Scripture to aid our understanding finds no comparison but the noonday light. "Thou shalt grope," says *Deuteronomy*, "in the noon, as grope the blind." And *Isaiah* (xvi. 3), "Make thy shadow as the night in midday." "Tell me," says the *Canticle*, "where thou liest at midday" (i. 6). This is the darkness which Saint Dionysius, following the Sacred Text, designates not as privation manifold, but as something positive: Caligo—Gnophos—araphel, and out of it he seems to make the very instrument of our knowing when he says that there is thrust out towards us a certain *caliginis divinae radius*, a gust of silence, a shaft of night. *Semitam meam circumsepsit*, says *Job* (xix. 8). "He hath hedged in my path round about, and I cannot pass," I am no longer subject to this transitory condition, "and in my way He hath set darkness." What is this *way*, this *path*, save what Jesus points when He says: I am the Way. Such was the sacred gloom that engulfed Moses on Sinai, which *Psalm* xcvi. 2 says is round about Him and how He has set it up as His display. That black point in the centre of the eye is what lets it see, as when we pray God "that the apple of His eye cease not towards us" (*Sam.* ii. 18).[1]

[1] *Ps.* xxx. 21. "Thou shalt hide them in the secret of Thy face." Mystery and evidence in one.

"Jesus is continually fixing His special gaze on me: spiritual, sorrowful, steadfast, and drowning in shadows of death, it pierces deep into my soul. And I, not able to turn away from it, do take this dreadful sad look, rife with a world of love and anguish. And His eyes bespeak again our union, what it expects of me, to

Darkness is what does away with limitation. For our relations with God we need something more essential than sense or mental faculties. All the works that God has made serve but to prosper our worship by endless litanies of negation.

To call God by name, to be delivered of that essential name in us whose utterance is our bounden duty, we must lend to justice the concurrence of our blindness, and to the working in us of the divine afflatus, that of our ignorance. In order to become acquainted with Being, it is our own being itself that we must place with Him in a kinship anterior to the morning, *ante luciferum*. We are definitely in the present. We are realising our formula. Everything in us becomes simultaneous, writ once for all on the "blue" of Eternity. We have

what it binds me. When two spouses question each other's eyes, they understand."

"Jesus took from me all that was mine and in its place put all that is His, so well that I seemed to have no more existence of my own. I was filled with His feelings, with His mind, His love of souls, His zeal for the glory of God. In a word, I was clothed in His essence." (*The Story of the German Franciscan Sister Maria Fidelis*, Desclée, 1932, pp. 250, 246.)

"By estate and grace of divine sonship and adoption justified, we live the life and mind of God Who is our mind and life: life and mind which rules us, enlivens us, and is the principle of our actions. The Christian's life is a life above lives and an essence above all essences. As the being and the excellence of a Christian consist in that he is a member of Jesus Christ, so the perfection of Christian actions (their very nature) should be in their being wrought by Jesus Christ alive and working in us as in His limbs" (Hugh Quarré, *Spiritual Treasure*, Bremond, vol. IX).

"Thy darkness shall be as the dayspring" (*Is.* lviii. 10).

"He will bring forth thy justice as the light, and thy judgment as the noonday" (*Ps.* xxxvi. 6).

betaken ourselves in nuptial mind. The new vision is but the development of our blissful night of Faith. Then the soul, giving ear, and forgetting her narrow house,[1] shall hear that word of promise : "I will espouse thee unto everlasting." [2]

[1] *Ps.* xliv. 11.

[2] *Hosea* ii. 19, 21 : "I will espouse thee and Me in faith. I will espouse thee in justice and in judgment."